ART DECO
IN AMERICA

EVA WEBER
ART DECO
IN AMERICA

Exeter Books

NEW YORK

A Bison Book

First published in USA 1985
by Exeter Books
Distributed by Bookthrift
Exeter is a trademark of Simon & Schuster, Inc.
Bookthrift is a registered trademark of Simon & Schu
New York, New York

ISBN 0-671-80804-4

Printed in Hong Kong

Page 1: Waylande Gregory, *Light Dispelling Darkness*, 1937.
Page 2: Raymond Hood, McGraw-Hill Building, New York City, 1931.
This page: *Gold Diggers of 1935* featured art deco style scenecraft.

CONTENTS

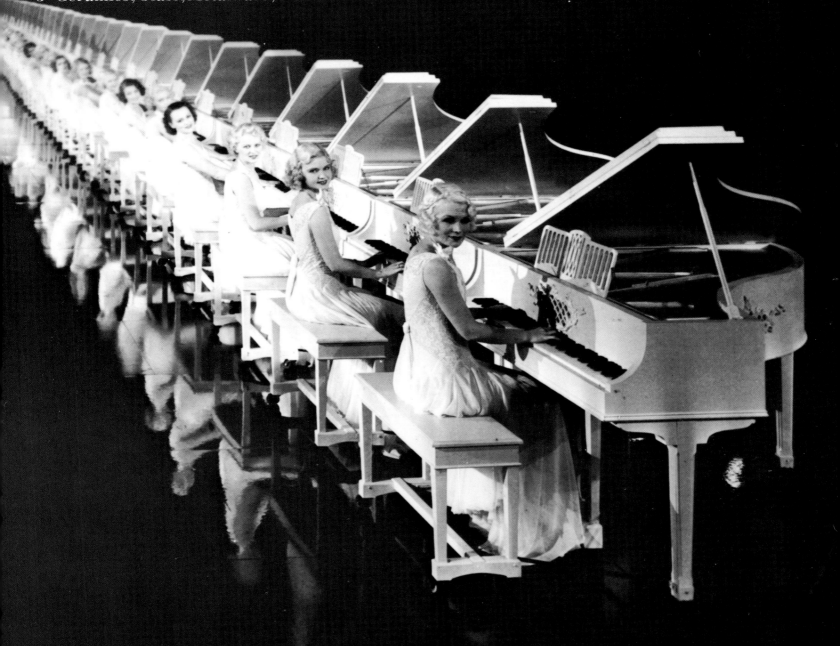

CHRONOLOGY

1900

Evans begins Knossos excavations in Crete
Freud, *Interpretation of Dreams*
First Zeppelin flight
Carry Nation begins temperance campaign in
 Kansas

1901

F. L. Wright delivers Chicago speech on 'The
 Art and Craft of the Machine'
First great oil strike near Beaumont, Texas
Auto speed record of a mile a minute is set in
 Brooklyn, New York
Olds, first mass-produced gasoline-powered
 car, is made in Detroit
President McKinley assassinated
Queen Victoria dies

1902

Stieglitz and others found Photo-Secession
Pierre and Marie Curie isolate radium
Willis Carrier invents air conditioning

1903

F. L. Wright, Larkin Building
Josef Hoffmann and others found Wiener
 Werkstätte
Frederick Carder founds Steuben Glass
First airplane flights by Wright Brothers
Henry Ford founds Ford Motor Company
First transcontinental auto trip

1904

F. L. Wright, Unity Church
Elie Nadelman begins decade-long exploration
 of ideal abstraction of forms

1905

Stieglitz opens Little Galleries, to become
 Gallery 291
Hoffmann and Wiener Werkstätte artists
 begin work on the Palais Stoclet in Brussels
Einstein publishes special theory of relativity

Left: Frank Lloyd Wright, window for
Arizona Biltmore Hotel, Phoenix, Arizona,
1927.

1906

Cezanne dies
First nickelodeon, regular movie theater, in
 Pittsburgh
Amundsen completes first ship passage of
 Northwest Passage
San Francisco earthquake

1907

Picasso's *Desmoiselles d'Avignon* begins
 cubism
Deutscher Werkbund founded
Lee De Forest begins experimental radio
 broadcasts from New York City studio

1908

Manhattan skyscraper skyline begins to form
 with 47-story Singer Building, following
 1902 20-story Flatiron Building
Isadora Duncan introduces her modern dance
 in New York and London
First round the world automobile race
Ford introduces Model T

1909

Brancusi, *Sleeping Muse*
Wright, Robie House
Marinetti, *Futurist Manifesto*
Diaghilev founds Ballets Russes
Bleriot flies English Channel
Perry reaches North Pole
Bakelite, early form of plastic

1910

Book on Wright's buildings and designs
 published in Berlin
Austrian Werkbund founded
Halley's Comet passes near earth
Mexican revolution begins
King Edward VII dies, ending Edwardian era

1911

Joseph Urban moves to the United States
Overbeck Pottery established in Indiana
Franz Boas, *The Mind of Primitive Man*
Hiram Bingham discovers Inca ruins at
 Macchu Picchu

First transcontinental flight by C. P. Rogers;
 air time 82 hours, 4 minutes
Amundsen reaches South Pole
Chinese revolution of Sun Yat-sen overthrows
 Manchu dynasty

1912

Duchamp, *Nude Descending a Staircase*
Newark Museum begins innovative program of
 industrial design exhibits
Head of Nefertiti found
Titanic sinks

1913

Armory show brings modern art to the US
Stanton Macdonald Wright and Morgan
 Russell develop synchromism
Psychologist John Watson develops be-
 haviorism
Domelre, first domestic electric refrigerator,
 made in Chicago

1914

Viennese modernist designer Paul Frankl
 arrives in New York
F. L. Wright, Midway Gardens
Cologne Werkbund exhibition – Austrian
 Pavilion by Hoffmann, Glass House by
 Bruno Taut, model factory by Gropius and
 Meyer
Sant'Elia's proposal for the 'City of the
 Future'
World War I begins

1915

Duchamp and Picabia arrive in New York,
 promote the machine aesthetic
Claude Bragdon, *Projective Ornament*
Panama Pacific international exposition in
 San Francisco
First transcontinental telephone talk by Bell
 and Watson

1916

Dada movement begins in Zurich
Pershing enters Mexico in pursuit of Pancho
 Villa
Rasputin murdered in Russia

1917

Strand makes pioneer machine aesthetic photo of automobile wheel assembly
Joseph Stella, *Brooklyn Bridge*
F. L. Wright, Barnsdall House
Man Ray experiments with airbrush painting
Mondrian starts *de Stijl* magazine
First jazz recording by Original Dixieland Jazz Band
Russian Revolution begins

1918

In *After Cubism*, Le Corbusier accuses modern movement of decorativeness
Leonard Woolley begins Assyrian excavations
Joyce publishes early parts of *Ulysses*
Astronomer Harlow Shapley discovers extent of Milky Way galaxy
Largest reflecting telescope in world installed at Mt. Wilson Observatory
World War I ends
Czar Nicholas and family assassinated

1919

Bauhaus founded at Weimar
Rena Rosenthal opens New York shop, Austrian Workshop
Kem Weber opens design studio in California
Solar eclipse supports Einstein's theory of relativity
First airship crosses Atlantic
Lenin founds Third International to wage worldwide revolution

1920

Goodhue's design wins architecture competition for Nebraska State Capitol
Arts Center founded in New York as clearinghouse for modern design ideas, has 6 galleries
Architectural League of New York adds medal in 'industrial art'
First commercial radio station organized, KDKA in Pittsburgh
Albert Michelson calculates first accurate measurement of a star, Betelgeuse
Prohibition amendment ratified
Women granted right to vote

1921

Man Ray and Moholy-Nagy begin making photograms, cameraless prints
Sheeler and Strand make film, *Mannahatta*

1922

Chicago Tribune Tower competition; second prize brings Saarinen to United States
F. L. Wright, Imperial Hotel; survives 1923 Tokyo earthquake
Urban organizes Wiener Werkstätte exhibit at Art Institute of Chicago; founds Werkstätte showroom in New York
Lozowick travels to Moscow, impressed with constructivists
Frankl opens New York gallery to sell own and imported designs
Tutankhamen's tomb discovered in Egypt
T. S. Eliot, *The Wasteland*
Mussolini becomes Italian prime minister

1923

Le Corbusier, *Vers une architecture*
Construction begins on New York's pioneer art deco building, Ralph Walker's New York Telephone
Georg Jensen opens New York outlet
Archipenko moves to the United States
Frazer's one volume version of *Golden Bough*
Kapek's *RUR* premieres in Prague, introduces robots
Elmer Rice, *The Adding Machine*
Hitler's Munich putsch fails and he is sent to prison where he writes *Mein Kampf*

1924

Erté begins exclusive contract to design covers for *Harpers Bazaar*
Congressional law makes Indians United States citizens

1925

Paris *Exposition Internationale des Arts Decoratifs et Industrials Modernes*
Ferrobrandt opens in New York, with Bouy as manager
Fitzgerald, *The Great Gatsby*
Kafka, *The Trial*
British scientist John L. Baird transmits first television image
Physicist Robert A. Millikan names 'cosmic rays,' discovered by Victor Hess in 1912
Darwin's evolutionary theory is challenged in Scopes monkey trial

1926

George Booth commissions Saarinen to design Cranbrook Academy of Art
Metropolitan Museum hosts loan exhibition from Paris exposition; opens permanent gallery of modern decorative arts
D. H. Lawrence, *The Plumed Serpent*
Robert Goddard's first liquid fuel rocket flight
Byrd and Bennett fly over North Pole
American Gertrude Ederle is first woman to swim English channel

1927

Macy's Art-in-Trade exposition of European and American art moderne, room of Frankl's skyscraper furniture, with installation designed by Lee Simonson
Machine-Age exposition in New York's Steinway Hall juxtaposes fine arts, design and machine parts
Buckminster Fuller designs Dymaxion House
Sheeler photographs Ford plant at River Rouge
Bel Geddes begins industrial design career with department store window displays; in 1930 he will have 40 assistants
Gutzon Borglum begins work on Mt. Rushmore
First part-sound film, *The Jazz Singer*
Lindbergh's New York-Paris nonstop flight in *Spirit of St. Louis*

1928

Macy's 'The First International Exposition of Art in Industry'; Lord & Taylor, B. Altman, and Abraham & Straus also host exhibits of modern design
Debut exhibit at American Designers Gallery, Inc. shows work by Deskey, Diederich, the Hoffmanns, Karasz, Reeves and Urban
Boas, *Primitive Art*
Mead, *Coming of Age in Samoa*
Amelia Earhart is first woman to fly Atlantic

1929

Metropolitan Museum's Architect and Industrial Arts exhibit includes rooms by Hood, Walker, Kahn, Saarinen, Urban, others
Ferriss, *The Metropolis of Tomorrow*
Museum of Modern Art founded, promotes European functionalist design
First Academy Awards, *Wings* is best picture
Astronomer Edwin Hubble confirms theory of expanding universe
Wall Street crash

1930

William Van Alen, Chrysler Building
Le Corbusier, Villa Savoye – a machine for living
The Chicago Workshops, an artists and designers co-operative modeled after Austrian Werkbund
Fortune magazine begins publication
Photographer Curtis concludes his 20-volume documentation, *The North American Indian*
Planet Pluto is discovered
Ernest Lawrence and staff invent cyclotron, an atom smasher

1931

Empire State Building, McGraw Hill Building, George Washington Bridge completed
Metropolitan Museum's 12th industrial design exhibit, works are more austere and rely more on mass production techniques
American Institute of Interior Designers founded
Influenced by Rohde, Herman Miller furniture company shifts to producing modern designs
Annual of American Design 1931 debates élite design vs mass production
Major exhibit of Indian tribal arts opens at New York's Grand Central Galleries
Martha Graham's modern dance, *Primi-Mysteries*
Aviators Wiley Post and Harold Gatty circle globe in record 8 days, 15 hours
Swiss physicist August Picard ascends by balloon 52,000 feet into stratosphere
Radio waves from space discovered, lead to radio astronomy

1932

Radio City Music Hall opens
Frankl calls Empire State Building a 'tombstone' to the zigzag era, and skyscrapers 'monuments to the greedy'
Museum of Modern Art's International Style exhibition
Norman Bel Geddes, *Horizons*
Huxley, *Brave New World*
Lindbergh kidnapping
Unemployment at 12 million

1933

Chicago Century of Progress Exposition

Nazis close the Bauhaus; Gropius, Moholy-Nagy and Mies van der Rohe will come to United States

Wiley Post's first solo flight around world

Einstein emigrates to United States

New Deal legislation passed in Roosevelt's '100 Days'

Prohibition ends

Hitler becomes chancellor of Germany

1934

Metropolitan Museum's Contemporary American Industrial Art exhibit shows influence of streamlined style

Museum of Modern Art's Machine Art exhibit explores beauty of industrial components

Philadelphia Art Alliance's Dynamic Design exhibit juxtaposes fine arts, commercial products, and industrial components

Carl Breer designs Chrysler 'Air Flow' automobile

Cocteau, *The Infernal Machine*

Graves, *I, Claudius*

Below: Ballroom by Schultz and Weaver, Waldorf Astoria Hotel, New York City.

1935

New Deal's Works Progress Administration begins operation

Russel Wright's *Modern Living* furniture line begins production

First practical helicopter developed in France

First experimental artificial heart developed by Dr. Alexis Carrel and Lindbergh

Board game MONOPOLY introduced

1936

F. L. Wright, Falling Water house

In New York, WPA establishes Design Laboratory headed by Rohde; board of advisers includes Deskey, Kahn, Lescaze, Loewy, Simonson, Russel Wright, and Lewis Mumford

British King Edward VIII abdicates to marry Wallis Simpson

Spanish Civil War begins

Berlin Olympics are Nazi showpiece

1937

Moholy-Nagy arrives in Chicago, sets up New Bauhaus in mansion provided by Marshall Field III

Golden Gate Bridge completed, longest in world to date

First successful jet engine tested in Great Britain

Amelia Earhart lost during flight over the Pacific

Airship *Hindenburg* explodes at Lakehurst, New Jersey

1938

Museum of Modern Art hosts exhibition of Bauhaus design

Orson Welles' *War of the Worlds* radio broadcast causes widespread panic

German scientists Otto Hahn and Fritz Strassen produce the elements barium and krypton by means of nuclear fission

Nazis occupy Austria, Czechoslovakia

1939

New York World's Fair, 'World of Tomorrow'

San Francisco Golden Gate Exposition

F. L. Wright, Johnson Wax building

Aiken and team begin construction of electromechanical computer; Atanasoff invents simple electronic digital calculating machine

Germans fly first jet plane, the Heinkel

World War II begins

Einstein sends Roosevelt letter proposing American atomic bomb project

FOUNDED BY ADOLPH SIEROTY

INTRODUCTION

Of all the decorative arts styles, art deco was perhaps the most eclectic, drawing as it did on a wide variety of historical and contemporary sources. Referring to the modernistic decorative style that was an important design trend in European and American arts and architecture in the decades between the two world wars, 'art deco' as a title actually dates from the 1960s, when the style began to enjoy a revival. During its heyday in the 1920s and 1930s, art deco was known as the *style moderne*. The current name of 'art deco' derives from the pivotal 1925 Paris *Exposition Internationale des Arts Decoratifs et Industrials Modernes* at which finely worked French furniture and other household accessories made for the luxury trade gained international recognition and are known to have significantly influenced both European and American designers.

The art deco movement affected all aspects of design, including architecture, interior design, furniture, industrial design, fashion, crafts production and graphics. It bore close affinities to and paralleled avant-garde developments in painting and sculpture. An embodiment of the machine age, art deco reflected the recent decades of rapid technological advance and an aesthetic appreciation of mechanical production. Art deco fostered collaboration between the arts and industry, and relied as well on the mass production of its designs. The art deco artists and designers experimented with novel and synthetic materials, and innovative construction techniques. They explored and adapted representations of the machine. A stylized and sometimes allegorical celebration of modern technological marvels – the automobile, the train, the airplane, electricity, telecommunications, radio, skyscrapers, bridges and related manifestations of contemporary life – was a frequent feature of architectural relief sculpture and murals. Even the idealized human figures were often abstracted to such a degree that they resembled human machines or robots.

Left: Claude Beelman, Eastern Columbia Building, Los Angeles, 1930.
Right: William Van Alen, Chrysler Building, New York City, 1930.
This was the archetypal American art deco skyscraper.

The art deco style pervaded the American market and art world through many routes. Even before the 1925 Paris Exposition, finely designed European consumer items in the modernistic style were available for sale in selected New York department stores. Major merchandisers, such as Macy's, also hosted exhibitions of the new applied arts in the mid-1920s. Museums also introduced

Above: Timothy Pfleuger, Paramount Theater, Oakland, Calif., 1931.

art deco design to the public. Beginning in 1923, New York City's Metropolitan Museum of Art began to purchase modern European decorative arts items. And in 1926, the Metropolitan displayed an exhibit of selected items from the Paris exposition of the previous year; this show later traveled to other American cities.

In 1929, the Metropolitan Museum hosted its own exhibit of comparable work produced in the United States. Titled *The Architect and the Industrial Arts: An Exhibition of Contemporary Design*, the show's layout was planned by immigrant architect and designer Eliel Saarinen, and it featured a series of rooms with furniture

and accessories by leading American architect-designers. In 1934 in New York City, both the Metropolitan and the recently founded Museum of Modern Art organized significant exhibitions of modern design, this time reflecting the streamlined phase of art deco.

The press observed these exhibits and their innovative designs with great interest. Specialized architectural and interior design periodicals published images of recent designs and projects, familiarizing the professional community with the latest developments. Also important in disseminating the art deco style were various books written and published by its practitioners; notable among these were Hugh Ferriss' *The Metropolis of Tomorrow* (1929), Paul Frankl's *New Dimensions* (1928) and *Form and Re-Form* (1930), and Norman Bel Geddes' *Horizons* (1932). Posters, prints, magazines and books produced by graphic designers, illustrators and commercial artists familiarized the public with the new art style.

Numerous European designers immigrated to the United States to further influence American art deco, among them Saarinen, Paul Frankl, Joseph Urban and many others. A number of native-born Americans also traveled to Europe to study, and some of them stayed on, as did graphic designer E McKnight Kauffer, to develop important careers abroad.

By general consensus, the term 'art deco' has come to encompass three distinct but related design trends of the 1920s and 1930s. The first was what is frequently referred to as 'zigzag moderne' – the exotically ornamental style of such skyscrapers as the Chrysler building and related structures such as the Paramount Theater of Oakland, California. The word 'zigzag' alludes to the geometric and stylized ornamentation of zigzags, angular patterns, abstracted plant and animal motifs, sunbursts, astrological imagery, formalized fountains and related themes which were applied in mosaic, relief and mural form to the exterior and interior of the buildings, many of which were ziggurat-shaped (receding in progressively smaller stages to the summit).

The second manifestation of art deco was the 1930s 'streamlined moderne' style – a futuristic-looking aerodynamic style of rounded corners and horizontal bands known as 'speed stripes.' In architecture, these elements were frequently accompanied by porthole windows, extensive use of glass block, and flat roof tops. The third style, referred to as either 'international stripped classicism,' or, more simply 'classical moderne,' also came to the forefront during the depression era of the 1930s. This was a more conservative style, blending a simplified and monumental modernistic neoclassicism with a more austere form of geometric and stylized relief sculpture and other ornament, including interior murals. Many buildings in this style were erected nationwide through programs of the New Deal.

Although art deco in its many forms was largely perceived as thoroughly modern, it was strongly influenced by the decorative arts movements that immediately preceded it. Like art nouveau, art deco made liberal use of plant motifs, but instead of the sinuous, flowing, asymmetrical foliage of art nouveau, that of art deco was regularized into abstracted and repetitive patterns. Like the Viennese craftspeople of the Wiener Werkstätte (a number of whom ended up in the United States), art deco designers worked with exotic materials, geometricized shapes and colorfully ornate patterns. And like the artisans of the Arts and Crafts Movement both in England and the United States, art deco designers considered it their mission to transform the domestic environment through well-designed furniture and household accessories. Although the Arts and Crafts Movement repudiated machine production of goods, art deco generally supported it.

An important link between the American Arts and Crafts Movement and the art deco designers was the versatile architect and designer Frank Lloyd Wright, who promoted the machine production of furniture and related items long before it was fashionable to do so, whose innovations in architectural and furniture design pioneered the use of abstract geometric ornament, who produced strikingly original buildings in the Mayan and streamlined styles, and whose ideas ón the symbolic

function of architecture and design were later echoed by art deco practices.

The revolutionary modern art movements centered in Paris during the early years of the twentieth century also had a lasting impact on art deco. Foremost among these was cubism, with its characteristic geometric stylization and fragmentation of images. Related movements also contributed – the orphism or synchromism of Sonia Delaunay and others brought vivid color to the geometric shapes of cubism; futurism celebrated speed, the machine, and the city; and constructivism experimented with new materials and mandated art to facilitate social progress. Many Americans were first directly exposed to the latest European modern art movements at the 1913 New York City Armory Show, and during its later travels to Chicago and Boston. The impact of this exhibition was far-reaching. Subsequent work produced by many leading American painters, sculptors and photographers was influenced at least to some degree by the abstraction and stylization practiced by Picasso, Matisse and Brancusi – tendencies that were paralleled in art deco design.

Below: Constantin Brancusi, *Sleeping Muse*, 1909-11.

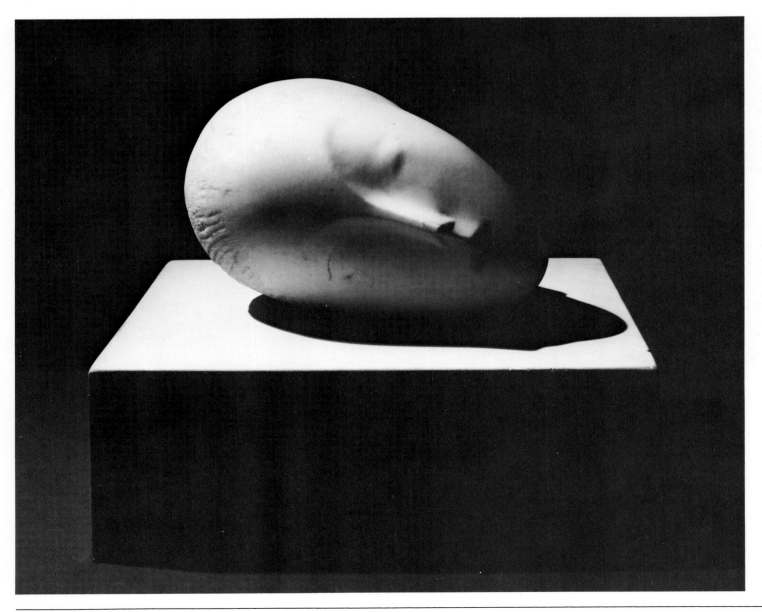

Above: Parkinson and Parkinson, Bullock's Wilshire, Los Angeles, 1928.
Right: Bullock's Wilshire, mural on port-cochere ceiling. Transportation as an essential art deco theme.

And just as leading modernist artists turned to primitive and ancient art for inspiration, so also did art deco designers. For example, sculptor Paul Manship incorporated motifs and techniques from Minoan and archaic Greek art, while other designers and architects adapted motifs from Egyptian and Assyrian art, recently newsworthy again because of new archaeological discoveries — the most spectacular of which was the 1922 opening of King Tutankhamen's tomb. The use of decorative motifs from these early cultures by art deco involved some degree of abstraction, adaptation and recombination with design elements from other sources. There were some spectacular movie palaces built in these decades that utilized, for instance, Egyptian motifs uniformly throughout the interior. Despite the resemblance to flamboyant art deco interiors, however, such a design scheme should really be considered as Egyptian Revival rather than art deco.

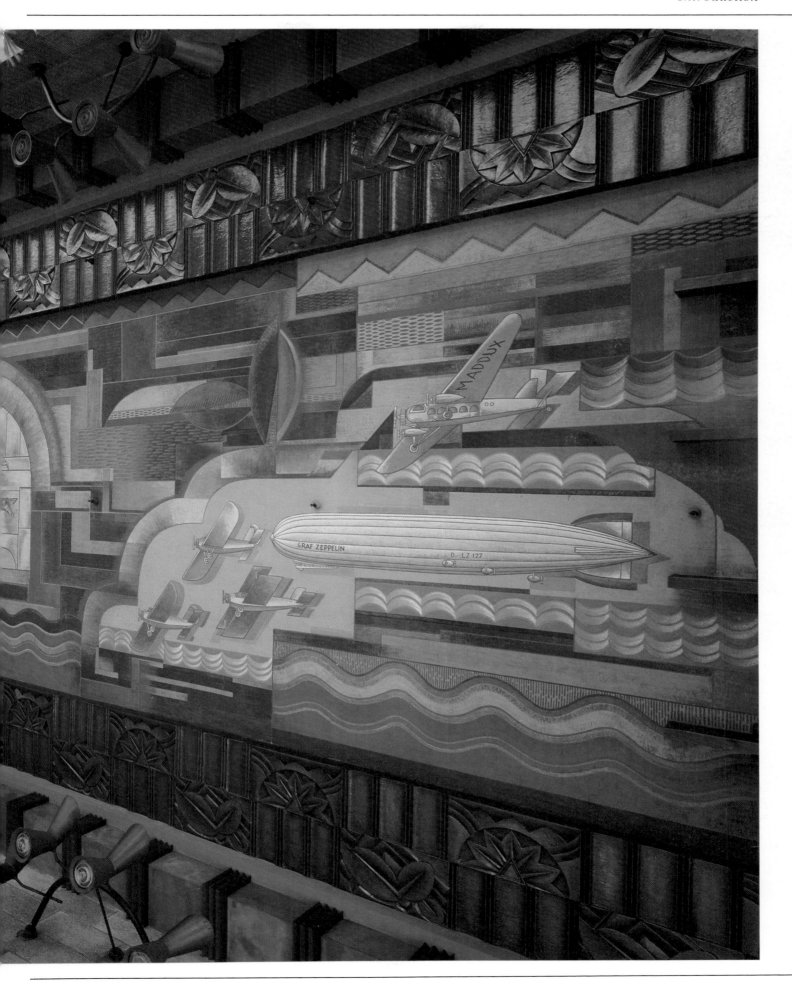

In the spirit of nationalism so prevalent during the 1920s, American art deco designers also sought out historical design motifs indigenous to the new world. American Indian art, with its geometric stylization and sophisticated patterns, was appreciated and collected by a number of important modernist artists and designers. Although this art was initially accessible only in ethnological collections, in 1931-1932 a major New York exhibition of American Indian tribal arts at Grand Central Art Galleries presented the aesthetic qualities of this type of art to a larger audience. Indeed, the new attention focused on American Indian art instigated a resurgence in the popularity of such items as ceramics, woven textiles and handmade jewelry. The 1928 American publication of anthropologist Franz Boas' pioneering and profusely illustrated book *Primitive Art*, which concentrated on the art of the Northwest Coastal Indians, not only helped to foster a wider appreciation of America's 'primitive arts,' but also provided a useful source book for designers.

Further native sources for art deco design were the pre-Columbian arts and architecture of Mexico and Central America. Frank Lloyd Wright drew on Mayan and Aztec temples as antecedents, beginning with his 1904 United Church and continuing with his texture block buildings and residential house of the 1920s. Following his example, Aztec style art deco became a significant factor in California architecture of the 1920s and 1930s. Another influence on the geometric patterning of art deco may have been a 1923 design book (published in New York in 1927) by Mexican artist Adolfo Best-Maugard. As a student, Best-Maugard had recorded primitive designs for Franz Boas, and had later exhibited in New York.

Above left: Paul Frankl, brass and bakelite mantel clock designed for Warren Telechron Company, circa 1930.
Above right: Jules Bouy, iron mantelpiece for Ferrobrandt, 1925-28.
Below and opposite: *Gold Diggers of 1933.*

A striking affinity existed between the stepped-back or ziggurat style skyscraper, and the stepped Mexican pyramids. And the simplified monumental forms of some of the architecture of the 1930s New Deal programs, notably some of the bridge pylons and dam piers, also

Above: Louis Sullivan, National Farmer's Bank, Owatonna, Minnesota, 1908. This was a prototype for art deco architectural ornament.

resembled pre-Columbian structures. A more contemporary Mexican influence on art deco in the United States came from the painters of the revolutionary Mexican muralist movement. Not only were such leading artists as Diego Rivera, David Alfaro Siqueiros and José Clemente Orozco granted major American commissions, which they executed using American assistants, but their socially pointed and formally stylized designs had an immeasurable impact on the New Deal muralists who decorated numerous civic structures, many of them in the classical moderne style, during the depression era. Such a cult developed around the Mexican muralists that many politically radical artists considered it an essential part of their artistic education to travel and study in Mexico.

An interest in yet another aspect of primitive art was fostered by the Harlem Renaissance – an extraordinary flowering of Afro-American culture and arts during the 1920s. Widespread appreciation of jazz, the quintessential music of the 1920s, was accompanied by a fascination with the stylized sculpture, masks and other arts of black Africa. Such motifs were not only explored by black American artists, but were also adapted by art deco designers such as Winold Reiss for fashionable restaurant and nightclub interiors.

Many of the primitive and historical styles adapted by art deco were made available at the same time to a mass

audience of unprecedented size through the new medium of film. Such early extravaganzas as D W Griffith's 1916 *Intolerance* and Cecil B DeMille's 1923 version of the *Ten Commandments* helped to popularize mid-east design motifs, and could also have influenced art deco designers, as well as their clients. Undoubtedly there was some degree of cross-fertilization between art deco design and film. German film director Fritz Lang was inspired by a glimpse of the New York skyscraper skyline to create that masterpiece of art deco scenecraft, *Metropolis*. This film, which subsequently premiered in New York in 1927, in turn probably had some impact on public acceptance and appreciation of art deco design ideas. As in the film, the use of art deco design to suggest the paradoxical merging of a futuristic world with the contemporary world underlay much of the self conscious modernism of art deco, not only in its flamboyant manifestation during the 1920s, but also in its streamlined phase of the 1930s, culminating in the 1939 New York World of Tomorrow exposition.

Further influences on art deco design came from the theater. Indeed, a number of important art deco designers, among them Joseph Urban and Norman Bel Geddes, had also worked as stage designers. The colorful and exotic costumes and sets created by Leon Bakst for the 1909 Paris performances of Sergei Diaghilev's Ballets Russes had a significant influence on art deco design. Closer to home, theater also influenced art deco's dramatic lighting effects – as seen in the exterior night illumination of skyscrapers and other art deco buildings, as well as in the innovative and spectacular use of neon

Left: Claude Beelman, Eastern Columbia Building, Los Angeles, 1930. The building was sheathed in blue-green terra cotta tiles.
Below: Buzz's Skelly service station, Colorado Springs.

and fluorescent light at the Chicago and New York world's fairs of the 1930s. The ornate entrances and lobby areas of zigzag style buildings were achieved by the incorporation of interior design motifs that were also used in theaters.

American art deco design was not confined only to the sophisticated urban centers of the East and West Coasts. The bustling commercialism and prosperity of the 1920s resulted in building booms elsewhere in the nation. Important examples of zigzag style architecture can be found in such cities as Syracuse, New York, and Pittsburgh, Pennsylvania. And cities that were actually developed during the 1920s – notably, newly oil-rich Tulsa, Oklahoma, and Miami Beach in the midst of the Florida land boom – had accumulated remarkable enclaves of art deco architecture by the end of the 1930s. And the

federally-sponsored New Deal construction projects helped to spread the more conservative art deco architecture of classical moderne throughout the nation in the form of governmental and civic buildings. The least ornate of the architectural manifestations of art deco, streamlined moderne made its widest impact on the American landscape through its gas stations, diners and other roadside amenities, although it was also seen in some major commercial and industrial commissions – notably Frank Lloyd Wright's Johnson Wax Building, and at the New York World's Fair. In the area of domestic architecture, it was a popular choice for Florida's and California's tropical deco apartment buildings and hotels.

While the Paris-influenced, craft-oriented style of art deco furniture and household accessories of the 1920s tended to be directed toward a more exclusive clientele,

Below: The film set of *Metropolis* (1926) was inspired by Fritz Lang's shipboard view of Manhattan's skyscraper skyline.

Right: The streamlined style's futuristic implications were effectively exploited in *Things to Come* (1936).

Left: The tropical deco architecture in southern Florida led to the designation of Old Miami Beach as an historical district.
Above: Shreve, Lamb & Harmon, Empire State Building, New York, 1931. It ended the era of zigzag style skyscraper construction.

and in design was more luxuriant and individualistic, such symbolic capitalism fell out of favor during the depression decade. In contrast, the household articles of the 1930s were created specifically for a mass audience, and their design was based on accessibility, ease of manufacture, and market appeal. During the 1930s, the streamlined style, the brainchild of the newly emergent industrial design movement, came to dominate the design of trains, cars, domestic appliances and household accessories. Its implications of speed and efficiency were expressions of the industrial designers' strong interests in social engineering and of their desire to create a New American utopia of the machine age and the consumer. These ideas sought both escape from and practical solutions to the grim realities of the depression. Not coincidentally, the homogenous streamlined style of the classical moderne architecture of the New Deal bore close affinities to the official architecture of the rising European totalitarian states – which offered alternative solutions to the social problems of the 1920s and 1930s. But in the United States it was finally World War II and not utopian social solutions that brought an end to the economic problems of the depression. And with World War II, the art deco style lost its distinctive configurations and energy.

1
SOURCES AND PARALLEL TENDENCIES: PAINTING, SCULPTURE AND PHOTOGRAPHY

The American art deco style of architecture and design incorporated ideas and motifs of early twentieth century modern art movements, especially cubism, and the related movements of synchromism, futurism, constructivism and precisionism.

Painting

After the turn of the century, the American art scene was one of relative stagnation compared to the ferment in European centers of culture. Academic conservatives who looked to the past for inspiration dominated the official United States art establishment. Between 1900 and 1913, almost every progressive American artist traveled to France to study. These temporary expatriates included Max Weber, Arthur B Carles, Morgan Russell, Patrick Henry Bruce, Alfred Maurer, Arthur B Dove, Marsden Hartley, John Marin, Charles Sheeler, Abraham Walkowitz, Charles Demuth, Stanton MacDonald-Wright, Andrew Dasburg, William Zorach, Marguerite Zorach, Thomas Hart Benton, Morton Schamberg, Joseph Stella, Oscar Bleumner and John Covert. Most of these artists returned to New York by the time of the first world war, bringing with them the first-hand lessons of European modernism.

These recent artistic developments were introduced to the American public by two primary means – the efforts of photographer and gallery director Alfred Stieglitz, and the astounding revelations of the 1913 Armory show. Beginning in 1908, Stieglitz mounted exhibits of work by pioneering European modernists Auguste Rodin, Henri Matisse, Paul Cezanne, Pablo Picasso, Henri Rousseau, Francis Picabia and Constantin Brancusi for relatively limited audiences and to generally unfavorable notices. Exhibitions at Stieglitz's Gallery 291 in New York City during the same years included such American modernists as Maurer, Hartley, Marin, Dove, Weber, Carles, Stella, Walkowitz, Bluemner, Georgia O'Keeffe and Elie Nadelman.

Left: Marcel Duchamp, *Nude Descending a Staircase, No. 2,* 1912.

But the earth-shaking event for the American public was the notorious Armory show that opened in New York City on 17 February 1913, and later traveled, in a truncated version, to Chicago and Boston. This mammoth exhibition of some 1600 items, three-quarters of which were by American artists, attempted to show the evolution of modern art since the late nineteenth century. The European section particularly became the focus of generally hostile and uncomprehending controversy. Marcel Duchamp's cubist-influenced *Nude Descending a Staircase, No. 2,* which one critic nicknamed the 'explosion in a shingle factory,' was the center of widespread ridicule. Nevertheless, the exhibit had an enormous impact. An estimated 600,000 people came to see it, and American collectors purchased some 300 works from it. After the initial public outrage, the mind of the public slowly began to accept and appreciate the ideas of modernism.

The pivotal modernist movement was that of cubism, which began in Paris in 1907 with Picasso's *Les Desmoiselles D'Avignon.* This landmark painting overturned the traditional ideas of artistic representation – the figures were abstracted into faceted and overlapping planes; one figure was simultaneously depicted from several viewpoints; and perspective was abandoned in favor of spatial ambiguity. Picasso derived these formal techniques from the example of African sculpture and from the theories of painter Paul Cezanne, who had insisted that the artist must 'treat nature in terms of the cylinder and the sphere and the cone.' Picasso, Georges Braque, Juan Gris, Fernand Leger and others continued to explore these ideas and techniques into the 1920s. As the initial structural experimentation lost momentum, cubism became more decorative in the hands of some artists; color came to play a greater role, and geometric stylization and faceted planes resolved themselves into rhythmic patterns.

Abstraction and geometric stylization, in repetitive and rhythmic patterns also became distinctive features of art deco design. The important contribution of Leger was his attention to cylindrical and curvilinear forms – in con-

Above: Max Weber, *Rush Hour, New York*, 1915.

trast to the more cubic and rectilinear shapes preferred by Picasso and Braque – as was his interest in machine-like forms and urban subject matter. These motifs also became important in art deco design.

American artist Max Weber was one of the earliest, beginning around 1911, to use cubist techniques and motifs in his work. Weber had returned to New York City in January 1909 after three years of study in Paris, where he had become familiar with all the latest developments of modernism. His most cubist-type work was executed between 1915 and 1917, and it helped to introduce the style to the United States. Weber's 1912-1916 New York series, including *Chinese Restaurant* and *Rush Hour, New York*, displayed the essential characteristics of cubism: the geometric stylization; the fragmented planes and multiple points of view; and the rhythmic incorporation of triangles, zigzags, echoing parallel lines and curves. Art deco patterns frequently incorporated such geometric motifs. These inventive paintings by Weber also owed something to futurism with their effect of dynamic movement. Of further significance was Weber's choice of subject matter – his interest in the American scene and, in this case, the excitement of New York City's urban life. Weber shared other basic interests with the Paris cubists. He was among the first Americans to purchase African sculptures, and further extended this appreciation to distinctly American primitive art. In 1910, he published an important and influential article on pre-Columbian and American Indian art in Stieglitz's avant-garde journal *Camera Work*.

The early work of Man Ray (born in Philadelphia as Emmanuel Radenski) was also closely allied to cubist theory. Man Ray moved to New York City in 1908 to work in an advertising agency and later as an engineering draftsman. The techniques of commercial art learned at this time were later incorporated by Ray into his experiments in painting, sculpture and photography. Like Weber's, Man Ray's interpretation of cubism was in-dividualistic. His 1914 painting *A.D.1914* depicted soldiers stylized into tubular fighting machines, reminiscent of Leger's mechanomorphic people. This stylization of the human figure into almost machine-like forms also characterized art deco.

Following the Armory show, French modernists Marcel Duchamp, Albert Gleizes and Francis Picabia were active in New York, not only helping cubism to gain wider American acceptance, but also experimenting with works that explored, often in a playful fashion, the dynamics and aesthetics of the machine. Picabia completed a series of satirical 'object portraits,' in which a machine or machine parts represented a particular person; for example, a camera represented Alfred Stieglitz. In 1915, Man Ray began a lifelong friendship and collaboration with Duchamp. And in 1917, Ray pioneered the 'aerograph' painting by using an airbrush or spraygun to produce paintings incorporating such machine imagery as gear wheels. The airbrush technique, in which the canvas remained untouched by the human brush stroke, was an apt medium for the mechanistic subject matter. The use of the airbrush also became an integral part of art deco graphics and commercial illustration technique to produce a slick, stylized finish particularly appropriate to art deco imagery. After Man Ray moved to Paris in 1921 (returning to the United States only during the 1940s), he continued his modernistic experimentation in photography and other media.

Inspired by the new ideas presented at the Armory show, and by the examples of Duchamp, Picabia, Ray and others, many noted American modernists began to explore cubist techniques and use cubist motifs. Among

Below: Man Ray, *A.D. 1914*. 1914.

27

these Americans were Marsden Hartley, John Marin, Abraham Walkowitz, Henry Fitch Taylor, Arthur Davies, Marguerite Zorach, William Zorach, Alfred Maurer, H Lyman Säyen and Stuart Davis. As a movement, cubism was also important in that it gave rise to other movements significant to art deco – futurism, constructivism, synchromism and precisionism.

The celebration of the new machine age and of its dynamic energy was the main thrust of the Italian futurist movement, founded in 1909 with a manifesto by poet Filippo Marinetti. Sculptor Umberto Boccioni and painters Carlo Carra, Giacomo Balla and Gino Severini employed the cubist techniques of fragmented planes, combined with futurist elliptic and diagonal 'force lines,' or ray lines to suggest movement and energy. With their paintings, the futurists sought to express their enthu-

Below: Joseph Stella, *Skyscrapers*, 1922, third panel of the series, *New York Interpreted*.

siastic appreciation of the vitality and power of their contemporary industrial and urban world – with its fast cars, ocean liners, airplanes, communications networks and other technological marvels. The iconoclastic futurists, who attempted to depict movement in cinematic sequence, saw as their mission the destruction of 'the cult of the past,' and the elevation of a new aesthetic – 'the world's magnificence has been enriched by a new beauty: the beauty of speed . . . a roaring car that seems to ride on grapeshot is more beautiful than the *Victory of Samothrace*.' These attitudes and techniques found expression as well in American art deco design, which also celebrated modern means of transportation, and employed diagonal lines in its patterns to suggest dynamism.

American painter Joseph Stella spent the years 1902-1912 in Italy and France in close contact with the futurists. And Stella's work, after his return to the United States, bore close affinities to futurism. His 1917-1918 *Brooklyn Bridge* and his 1920-1922 *New York Interpreted* series (including *The Skyscrapers*) apotheosized modern technology and the modern metropolis. The bridge and the skyscrapers were revealed as central icons of modern American civilization. In these paintings, Stella used diagonal force lines, expressed by the structural elements of the bridge intermeshed with dramatic, almost mystical, beams of electric spotlights. In his painting of skyscrapers, the rays of light slashed across the severely geometric and monumental nighttime skyscrapers, coalescing energy, spirituality and materialism into an optimistic vision of American strength as expressed in its technology and architecture. Other American painters, notably John Marin and Charles Demuth, also superimposed diagonal ray lines over their representations of architecture to suggest a dynamic energy.

Futurist ideas and techniques – including the use of diagonal ray lines in architectural relief sculpture and interior ornamental patterns, the celebration of the dynamism of the machine and of the urban environment, and the use of dramatic nighttime lighting in the exterior illumination of art deco buildings and to create special, almost visionary effects at the Chicago and New York world's fairs of the 1930s – also became integral components of art deco design.

Synchromism was another offshoot of cubism important to art deco design. It was an innovative form of color abstraction in which geometric shapes – arcs, circles, wedges and bars – of intense complementary and contrasting colors were combined to form a rhythmic and lyrical whole. Synchromism was also unique in that it was the sole American-formulated modernist movement, complete with manifestos. Synchromism was founded in Paris in 1913-1914 by expatriate painters Stanton MacDonald Wright and Morgan Russell, who developed their theory of color painting after they had both attended classes taught by Canadian artist Ernest Percyval Tudor-Hart, who emphasized a system of color harmonies based on correspondences between hues and tonal sounds. At the same time in Paris, Robert Delaunay, Sonia Delaunay and František Kupka developed orphism, which is virtually indistinguishable from synchromism (an unresolved controversy still exists as to which group came to abstract color painting first). Synchromism, well publicized by Stanton MacDonald Wright's brother, obtained a number of American adherents before it lost momentum with World War I. Among those Americans who painted synchromist pictures were Thomas Hart Benton, Andrew Dasburg, Patrick Henry Bruce, Arthur B Frost Jr, Morton Schamberg and Joseph Stella.

The motifs of this early color painting – the abstract arcs, circles (or discs), wedges and other geometric shapes of contrasting and complementary colors – became popular features of art deco, particularly in the design of textiles and china, primarily through the agency of Sonia Delaunay. In 1913 she began to create such colorful geometric designs for textiles (of which she did over 2000 during the 1920s), fashionable clothing, furniture, rugs, ceramics, wallpaper, graphics, advertisements and books. Her designs were shown at the 1925 Paris exposition and met with international appreciation. A primary method by which Delaunay's designs were promulgated was through the technique of *pochoir* – a luxurious print-making medium using stencils to reproduce handpainted designs. In Paris, *pochoir* was used in limited edition books, high fashion magazines, expensive wallpapers, prints and in portfolios of design and decoration. Limited edition *pochoir* albums of colored art deco design motifs designed by Delaunay and others helped to spread the style internationally to all areas of the decorative arts.

From cubism, and strongly influenced by the machine imagery of Marcel Duchamp and Francis Picabia, developed still another indigenously American modernist art movement. Known variously as the cubist realists, the new classicists and the immaculates, the painters working in this style have recently become known as the precisionists. Precisionism, which encompassed the years from the first world war through the 1920s, applied cubist principles of geometric reductiveness but eliminated its planar fragmentation and spatial ambiguities to realistically portray architectural and technological subject matter – skyscrapers, grain elevators, factories, bridges, steamships, trains and, to a lesser degree, domestic architecture. The characteristic precisionist work was painted in a meticulous style that approached photographic clarity with its sharp-edged lines, clean smooth surfaces, simplified volumetric forms and subdued colors. These paintings ignored human and social issues, and concentrated instead on exploring the aesthetic forms and monumental qualities of distinctively American technology and architecture. Inanimate subject matter was endowed with a heroic quality and a sense of weighty permanence – a quality hitherto attributed almost exclusively to ancient, classical and European architecture and art.

Among the foremost precisionist works were Charles Demuth's *My Egypt*, an ironically titled painting of monolithic grain elevators; Charles Sheeler's 1931 *Classic Landscape*, a pristine view of the Ford Motor Company River Rouge Plant which Sheeler earlier had been commissioned to photograph; and Sheeler's 1939 *Rolling Power*, a painting of locomotive wheels and drive shafts that explored the formal relationship of the intercon-

Above: Elsie Driggs, *The Queensborough Bridge*, 1927.

nected machine parts. Demuth often incorporated futurist ray lines in his precisionist paintings, while Sheeler, who supported himself by working as a commercial photographer, also used photographs as studies for a number of his precisionist paintings.

A number of important American modernists executed works in the precisionist style. Among them were Georgia O'Keeffe, Louis Lozowick, Preston Dickinson, George Ault, Francis Criss, Stefan Hirsch, Niles Spencer, Ralston Crawford and Edmund Lewandowski. Elsie Driggs also produced precisionist paintings for a relatively short while. Her paintings of the Queensborough Bridge and of Pittsburgh celebrated the nation's industrial monuments, while exploring their idiosyncratic beauty by abstracting their geometric elements through dramatic cropping techniques akin to those used by photographers. While precisionism was not a formal art

Left: Stanton MacDonald-Wright, *Conception: Synchromy*, 1915.

movement, there was a community of interest among its practitioners based on their utilization of similar themes and techniques. And the sharp-edged geometric clarity of precisionism and its subject matter were also echoed in art deco geometric patterns, architectural relief sculpture and the New Deal murals of the 1930s.

Constructivism was yet another modernist movement that had considerable impact on developments in American art deco design. Constructivism emerged in the years after World War I, and was closely allied in intent to the Dutch *De Stijl* movement, French purism, and the German Bauhaus – all of these movements sought a more rational and orderly art derived from and reflecting machine technology. Constructivism arose in the Soviet Union after the Russian Revolution and was initially concerned with the deliberate organization of abstract, non-expressive and frequently geometric elements into a rational whole. A schism soon developed between those artists who believed that art necessarily had a spiritual content, and those who judged 'art for art's sake' as decadent and insisted that the sole purpose of art was to be socially useful. Those artists who rejected the rigid social utility stance broke off from the Soviet constructivists, and were assimilated into and contributed to international constructivism and other modernist movements. Among these artists were Wassily Kandinsky, Naum Gabo, Antoine Pevsner, El Lissitzky, Laszlo Moholy-Nagy, and Alexander Archipenko. Those who remained with the Soviet constructivists were eager to participate in the nation's reconstruction and in the creation of a new society following the Russian Revolution and the devastation of World War I.

Central to the Soviet constructivist movement was Vladimir Tatlin's doctrine of the 'culture of materials' which urged experimentation with and the utilization of those properties distinctive to industrial materials. This ideologically-based, utopian constructivism was essentially a production art that saw the differences between artist and engineer eliminated. It was an art validated only by the mass production of socially useful goods. Thus, Soviet constructivism's leading artists concentrated on such endeavors as graphic design, furniture design, clothing design, design of industrial interiors, textile design and stage design. Only in this way could art be integrated into the social environment.

American artist Louis Lozowick, who painted in a precisionist style in the 1920s, studied and traveled in Europe from 1919 to 1924. In Berlin, he came in close contact with a number of Russian expatriate artists who expressed great admiration for modern American technological and architectural achievements. This encouraged Lozowick to treat such American subject matter, in his paintings, as an optimistic symbol of the modern age. In 1922, he was persuaded to visit Moscow, from which he returned with a profound appreciation of constructivism. Although Lozowick himself was less political and utopian than the Soviet constructivists, he helped to introduce their ideas to the United States in his 1925 book, *Modern Russian Art*, and in various essays published in magazines.

Above: Louis Lozowick, *Machine Ornament*, 1925-27.

The constructivist influence exerted itself in Lozowick's series of ink drawings, *Machine Ornaments*, which were closely allied to El Lissitzky's *Prouns* (Projects for the New Art) and Fernand Leger's *Machine Elements* drawings. In these semi-abstract compositions of machine parts, Lozowick sought to combine art and industrial design in a way that would suggest a model for social order. In 1926, Lozowick incorporated these *Machine Ornaments*, in monumental scale, into the set design for a Chicago production of Georg Kaiser's play *Gas*, as well as into a fashion show set he designed for New York City's Lord & Taylor department store. For *Gas*, he also designed a constructivist stage set of platforms at various levels with movable parts and gears, stairs and towers arranged horizontally, vertically and diagonally to permit the actors to use biomechanic movement. (In Soviet constructivist theater, biomechanics referred to a choreography of movement in which the actors moved very precisely, like machine parts, in synchrony with the movable parts of the stage set.) In these ways, Lozowick sought to expose a larger American audience to constructivist principles.

Several aspects of constructivism were significant for American art deco. Its essential principles – particularly, the experimentation with industrial materials, the emphasis on mass produced items, the importance of designing for the total environment, and finally, the role of design in transforming society – had their greatest impact in the 1930s, on the development of the American industrial design movement and its promulgation of the streamlined style throughout the nation. American industrial designers – notably Norman Bel Geddes in his book, *Horizons* – clearly regarded the Russian experiment as an important prototype for their own rationale and activity. Experimentation with new materials was also a significant aspect in the design of other American art deco furniture and household accessories when such hitherto industrial materials such as steel, chrome, aluminum and plastics were innovatively used in new contexts, or were inventively combined for unusual effects.

During the 1920s and 1930s, painting in Canada also paralleled art deco tendencies, even though Canadian artists were even further removed from exposure to the European modernist movements than were their colleagues in the United States. For many Canadian avant garde artists, a trip to or period of study in New York was their sole contact with the international vanguard.

The first important twentieth century movement in Canadian painting began around 1912 with the formation of the Toronto-centered Group of Seven, whose members were Lawren Harris, JEH MacDonald, AY Jackson, Frank Johnston, Frank Carmichael, Arthur Lismer and Fred Varley. In order to develop a uniquely Canadian idiom, these artists concentrated on their country's distinctive landscapes, literally working in the wilderness while on a series of treks to the Arctic, the Rocky Mountains, the Pacific coast, the Maritime provinces and other Canadian sites. Several of the Group of Seven and their followers, Lawren Harris foremost among them, painted their northern landscapes in a broad decorative modernist fashion – with dramatically stylized, sculpturally modeled, rhythmically disposed and spiritually energized mountains, clouds and other natural elements. Such renderings clearly owed a considerable amount to the precepts of cubism, and also echoed the stylistic devices of art deco.

Lawren Harris was a leading figure in bringing modernism to Canada. In 1914 he organized and largely financed Toronto's Studio Building of Canadian Art, and in 1927 was responsible for arranging, again in Toronto, an important exhibition of modern art collected by the New York-based Société Anonyme. In the late 1920s, Harris himself became a member of the Société Anonyme, joining Marcel Duchamp, Francis Picabia, Alexander Archipenko, Max Weber and other avant-garde artists. In the 1930s and early 1940s, Harris' work entered a realm of pure abstraction that drew on the cubist and futurist techniques of intersecting geometric and curvilinear planes that also informed art deco patterns.

Other Canadian artists exploring similar modernist ideas and techniques included Ernest Baker, Jock MacDonald and Carl Schaefer. Perhaps the most experi-

mentally inclined of the early Canadian modernists was Bertram Brooker, who also worked as a commercial artist, as a book illustrator and as a writer. In addition to his stylized landscapes, Brooker also executed figural compositions incorporating cubist and futurist techniques. Another key figure of the Canadian avant-garde was west coast artist Emily Carr, who had studied in England and France. On her return to British Columbia, she developed an interest in and drew inspiration from west coast Indian art. But her primitivistic paintings were not well received in Vancouver and she virtually stopped painting. Some 14 years later, Carr's work was shown in Ottawa. The Group of Seven recognized her achievement, and subsequently encouraged her to resume painting. Her later work was strongly influenced by the monumental stylized forms depicted by Lawren Harris, and Carr executed decorative, dynamic, cubist-style landscapes with repeated zigzags formed by the contours of pine trees – a uniquely Canadian interpretation of a motif that in art deco design in the United States referred to lightning and symbolized energy.

Sculpture

Avant-garde sculpture of the 1920s and 1930s was also important to art deco design. Not only did it reflect the ideas of cubism and the other modernist movements, but the sculpture itself was frequently incorporated into art deco architectural settings, as at Rockefeller Center and at the world's fairs of the 1930s. And in the form of carved or cast decorative relief panels, tiles and figures, sculpture was integrated into the total design of art deco buildings in the zigzag style and in the classic moderne style. The architectural sculpture enriching building facades, entrances and lobbies was an essential and distinctive feature of the art deco style.

The most successful American sculptor of the art deco era was Paul Manship. He represented a more conservative trend in sculpture and must be considered a transitional figure between the beaux arts tradition and modernism. Manship's works, most of them cast in bronze, were objects of sophisticated craftsmanship and highly refined finish, verging on preciosity. Based on antique prototypes of mythological figures, a subject also popular in the nineteenth century, his sculpture drew their characteristic stylization not from the abstracting tendencies of cubism, but from the example of bronze age Mediterranean art. Along with an emphasis on linear elegance expressed in stylized hair and draperies and a clarity of contour resulting from a pictorial mode of composition, Manship oriented his sculptural elements frontally so that they resembled freestanding relief sculpture.

Awarded the coveted American Prix de Rome in 1909, Manship bypassed the obvious artistic mecca, Paris, to study in Rome. While there, he became familiar with Pompeiian frescoes, the decorative figures in antique vase paintings, and elegant statuettes from the Roman era. He was greatly impressed by archaic Greek sculpture and even traveled to Greece to study it first-hand. His 1924 *Diana* and *Actaeon* groups were decoratively and rhythmically stylized in archaic Greek fashion. Further travels around the Mediterranean also allowed him to become familiar with Egyptian, Minoan and Assyrian art, all of which had some effect on his sculpture, as they did on art deco architecture and design. Probably Manship's best-known sculpture is his monumental gilded bronze *Prometheus* at Rockefeller Center's focal fountain. The other, lesser known art deco sculptors and designers who produced stylized fauns and other mythological figurines in profusion were undoubtedly inspired by Manship's example.

Similar concerns informed the work of W Hunt Diederich, who concentrated on elegant stylized animals such as gazelles, greyhounds and horses. A member of a wealthy Hungarian family, the versatile Diederich was the grandson of American painter William Morris Hunt and

the grandnephew of architect Richard Morris Hunt. Following an education in Rome and Paris, he studied sculpture at the Pennsylvania Academy of Fine Arts.

Diederich's sculptural works also emphasized, as Manship's did, the two-dimensional, frontal aspect of their composition. Unlike Manship, though, Diederich was willing to apply these design principles to household accessories as well. He produced metalwork animal-style candelabra, firescreens and weathervanes, as well as ceramics painted with similar motifs. Some of Diederich's art deco geometric motifs were also based on the folk art (carvings and embroidery) of his native Hungary. Designer Winold Reiss made similar use of folk sources.

Folk art, this time American, was also an absorbing interest of the immigrant sculptor Elie Nadelman, whose refined, curved tubular figures and stylized abstract heads were an important antecedent for the women

Below: Paul Manship, *Dancer and Gazelles*, 1916. Manship and Nadelman also created art deco garden sculptures for the wealthy.

Opposite above left: Lee Lawrie, Rockefeller Center architectural relief, 1937, at the 14 West 49th Street entrance.
Opposite above right: Waldorf Astoria ballroom decorative detail. Fauns and other mythological beings were a popular art deco theme.
Opposite below: Paul Manship, *Prometheus*, Rockefeller Center. The Center marked an ambitious attempt to integrate sculpture.

depicted by leading fashion illustrators in the pages of sophisticated fashion magazines. Indeed, Nadelman's first patron was Helena Rubinstein, who commissioned a number of his elegant marble heads for her beauty salons. During the years 1904-1914 in Paris, Nadelman had attempted to achieve an ideal abstraction with his 'Researches in Volumes and Accord of Forms'; in fact, he was convinced that he and not Picasso had first discovered the principles of cubism.

Below: Hildreth Meiere, medallion of Comedy and Tragedy, Radio City Music Hall, Rockefeller Center.

During his stay in Paris, American painter Max Weber was among the first to experiment with cubist sculpture. His 1915 *Spiral Rhythm* combined cubism's volumetric solids with curves derived from Umberto Boccioni's futurist works. Weber ended his sculptural exploration of these techniques in 1915 and his work, although shown in New York, apparently had little effect on American developments in modern sculpture. Other Americans who studied in France also produced work incorporating cubist ideas. Alice Morgan Wright, in Paris from 1910 to 1912, produced figural works in cubist style. And Eugenie Shonnard, who studied with Rodin, subsequently produced a series of simplified volumetric statues of New Mexico's Indians. In their block-like, hierarchic appearance, her works resembled ancient Egyptian pharaonic statuary.

Perhaps the greatest influence on modernist American sculpture was exerted by Ukrainian-born Paris artist

Above: W Hunt Diederich, chandelier, circa 1920-30, wrought iron.
Above right: Theodore Roszak, *Airport structure*, 1932, copper, aluminum, steel and brass.

Alexander Archipenko, who came to live in the United States in 1923. From about 1911 on, Archipenko had made figural cubist sculptures in which the body was analytically reorganized into angular geometric planes. He also pioneered the revival of polychromy – the use of color – in sculpture. Many of his color effects were gained by using a variety of materials – such as bronze, iron, glass and wood – together in one work. In addition, he experimented with such industrial materials as highly polished aluminum and chromium to achieve machine-like surfaces. Besides his innovative polychromy and the inventive use of new materials, Archipenko in the 1940s explored the possibilities of light sculpture, in which plexiglass constructions were illuminated from their interior.

Obviously, fine art and art deco shared common concerns during the 1920s and 1930s, as art deco designers also explored the effects of color in architecture and the use of new materials in furniture design, as well as dramatic lighting effects.

Among American sculptors exploring the machine aesthetic, Theodore Roszak was the most notable. His 1932 *Airport Structure*, resembling a functional machine and executed in a variety of industrial metals – aluminum, brass, copper and steel – was a product of engineered design and the use of industrial tools and techniques. Yet,

the sculpture was intended as an object of aesthetic beauty, as were the figural works of other modernists. Familiar with constructivist precepts, Roszak emphasized the democratic essence of his works by offering to reproduce any of them in limited editions, thus lowering the cost to the consumer.

The exploitation of streamlined motifs with their resonances of efficiency and speed by the industrial designers of the 1930s was echoed by Wharton Esherick's highly polished 1932 aluminum sculpture, complete with art deco-style setbacks, speed stripes and a dramatically lunging forward silhouette that created an illusion of movement, as streamlined items also sought to.

Artist Rutherford Boyd approached his abstract parabolic sculptures much as industrial designers tackled their commercial assignments. Interdisciplinary research and mathematical computations – with the goal of discovering and articulating universal geometric principles – resulted in Boyd's streamlined sculptures. During the late 1930s, he also explored the possibilities of designing with light, and began to test such materials as translucent alabaster, marble, lucite, polished aluminum and mirrors for their absorbent and reflective qualities. The resulting sculptures, illuminated from within, housed artificial light sources in their bases. In his attitude toward the unification of art and technology, Boyd paralleled the interests of the constructivists, as well as of art deco designers.

An important pioneering American modernist sculptor who produced both cubist and constructivist works was John Storrs. Born in Chicago, Storrs studied sculpture

Above: Wharton Esherick, *Speed*, 1932, aluminum.
Right: John Storrs, *Stone Panel With Black Marble Inlay*,
cast stone and black marble.

and architecture in the United States, Paris and Berlin,
before becoming Rodin's favorite student from 1912 to
1914. Storrs lived for the rest of his life in France, with
frequent trips back to Chicago and New York. The versatile Storrs produced stylized cubist sculptures such as
his 1920 polychromed *Pieta* and the 1925 *Gendarme
Seated*. At the same time he explored more abstract
themes with such works as his 1917-1919 *Stone Panel
With Black Marble Inlay*. His incorporation of such
cubist motifs as curves, sharp angles and zigzags in
shallow relief, and his use of a variety of materials and
colors in one work predated similar developments in art
deco architectural ornament. Storrs also was an inno-
vator in using unusual metals and other materials. His
1924 *Forms in Space* combined aluminum, brass, copper
and wood. This and a number of similar 'skyscraper'
sculptures resembled simplified architectural models and
reflected, as well, the skyscraper motif so popular in
1920s art deco design.

Storrs' use of the zigzag and other geometric motifs was
influenced in part by American Indian art. Storrs greatly
admired Indian crafts, and possessed an impressive personal collection of Navaho blankets, pottery and other
decorated items. During the art deco years, a number of
American modernists collected Indian art.

Frank Lloyd Wright was openly appreciative of not just
pre-Columbian architecture, but also the arts of the

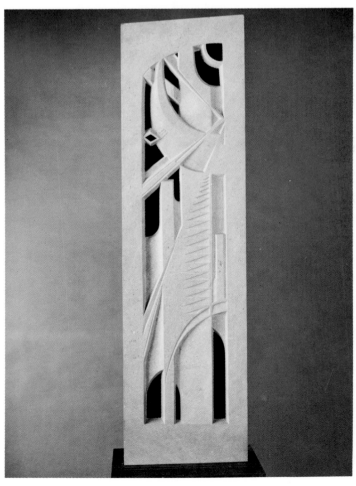

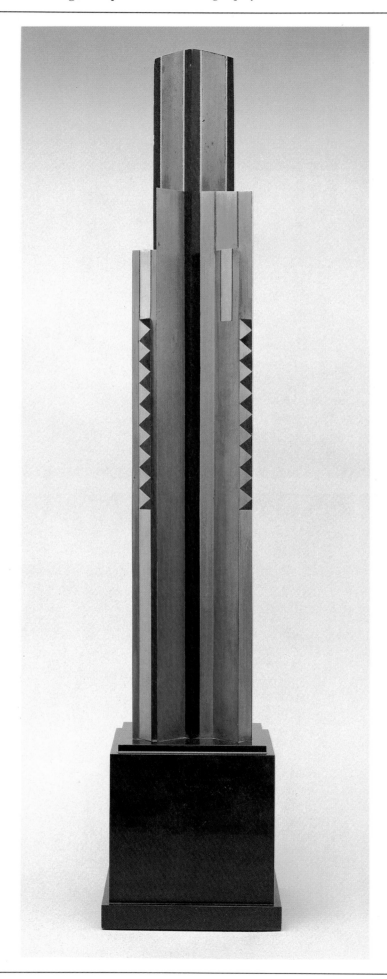

American Indians. In 1924 in connection with his Nakoma Country Club project, Wright created the terra cotta sculptures, later cast in bronze, of *Nakoma* and *Nakomis* which were obviously inspired by the American Indian. The art deco flavor of these stylized, rhythmic, cubist-influenced works underlines Wright's central importance to the development of American art deco design. As early as 1913, Wright designed art deco-style figurative facade sculptures for his Chicago Midway Gardens project. These sculptures were executed and cast by Wright's artistic collaborator on the project, Alfonso Iannelli.

Isamu Noguchi's sculpture also encompassed two distinct strains of the art deco era – the cubist and the constructivist. His 1929 chrome-plated bronze head of Buckminster Fuller, completed after Noguchi's return from Paris where he had worked as Brancusi's assistant, incorporated the simplification and stylization seen also in Brancusi's work. His use of an industrial material to give the head a gleaming, machine-like appearance with a polished surface that reflected and distorted the head's surroundings, resulted in a fragmented cubist effect.

Stylized, mask-like heads, reminiscent of primitive, Egyptian and archaic Greek sculpture, were a popular motif during these years. A wide variety of such heads were produced – among them, John Storrs' 1919 *Egyptian Head*, Elie Nadelman's 1909 *Abstracted Head* that was the precursor of Brancusi's *Muses*, Gaston Lachaise's 1928 nickel-plated bronze head, William Zorach's 1940 black porphyry head of Christ, and Sargent Johnson's numerous terra cotta African and Afro-American heads. Similar stylized heads appeared in art deco fashion illustrations and posters. In their simplified and depersonalized form, the sculptured heads frequently emanated an almost magical sense of power, similar to the effect of ethnographic masks.

Noguchi's Buckminster Fuller head, in any case, was an apt evocation of the visionary designer who was himself an influential figure during the streamlined phase of art deco. The Fuller head also bore a close affinity to a major American icon also created in the late 1920s – the Academy Award, or 'Oscar.' This gold statuette, designed by art director Cedric Gibbons and cast by sculptor George Stanley, had a similar, simplified, stylized head and body with a glittering, machine-like finish. This imagery of 'supermen,' based on classical and neo-classical prototypes, was to continue in the New Deal architectural sculpture and murals of the 1930s.

Noguchi's first major commission was a large facade sculpture for Rockefeller Center's Associated Press Building in 1938. Executed in ten tons of stainless steel, the sculpture celebrated stylized, heroic newspaper workers – dynamic reporters, photographers and type-setters. At the same time, Noguchi was working in a more abstract, constructivist vein. His 1933 competition design, *A Bolt of Lightning – A Memorial to Benjamin Franklin*, was composed of a giant key supporting a zigzag stainless steel lightning bolt, topped by a steel tube kite. This sculptural use of industrial materials, in combina-

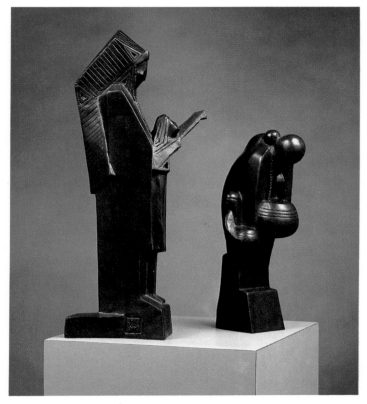

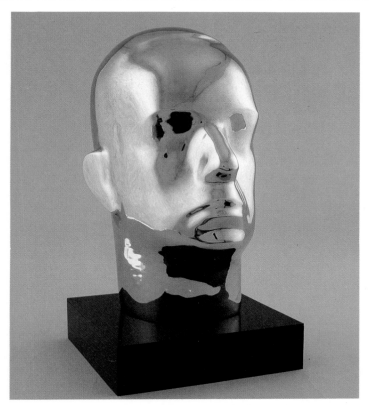

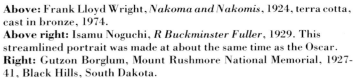

Above: Frank Lloyd Wright, *Nakoma and Nakomis*, 1924, terra cotta, cast in bronze, 1974.
Above right: Isamu Noguchi, *R Buckminster Fuller*, 1929. This streamlined portrait was made at about the same time as the Oscar.
Right: Gutzon Borglum, Mount Rushmore National Memorial, 1927-41, Black Hills, South Dakota.

tion with the popular art deco zigzag imagery was in the mainstream of art deco practice. The actual sculpture was not constructed until 1984, more than 50 years after its inception.

Another important commission of the 1930s was Noguchi's *Chassis Fountain*, incorporating oversize automobile parts, for the streamlined Ford Motor Company pavilion at the New York World's Fair. This sculpture celebrated the unity of art and technology, a primary concern of the 1930s industrial design movement.

Gutzon Borglum's colossal sculpture, the Mount Rushmore National Memorial in South Dakota, incorporates a number of significant art deco concerns spanning two decades. First proposed in 1923, the project was approved by the national and state governments in 1925. Work was actually begun on the granite surface of Mount Rushmore in 1927, finally reaching completion in 1941. Done in an academic neoclassical style, the faces of the four presidents – George Washington, Thomas Jefferson, Abraham Lincoln and Theodore Roosevelt – are about 60 feet tall, twice the height of the Egyptian sphinx at Giza. The Rushmore Memorial represented the strong current of American nationalism that pervaded the 1920s and 1930s – pride in American technological superiority and the development of distinctly American expressions in the decorative arts and architecture as well as in jazz music and literature. American wealth and agriculture in the 1920s was also a source of nationalistic pride.

Above: Cedric Gibbons, designer, *Oscar*, circa 1929.

Mount Rushmore's sheer monumentality echoed the insistence on American architectural achievements as equal to the monuments of the ancient and classical past. The process of Borglum's sculpting the Mount Rushmore Memorial brought together that dynamic triad of man, machine and nature so prevalent in art deco imagery. In the epic task of blasting out the living rock of the mountain with dynamite and jackhammer, the heroic artist became himself one of those classically idealized laborers seen so frequently in New Deal murals and sculpture. During the depression years, much of the federally-sponsored architecture exhibited a similar classicistic monumentality, evoking a reassuring sense of permanence. The governmental participation in the Rushmore project (it paid about 84 percent of the total cost of some $1,520,000) also predated governmental sponsorship of arts and architecture during the New Deal programs of the 1930s.

Photography

In the early decades of the twentieth century, photography made impressive advances toward recognition as a fine arts medium. And during the art deco era, photographers incorporated and contributed to visual techniques expressing the tenets of modernism, particularly of cubism and its derivative movements. In a way unparalleled by painting and sculpture, which catered to an elite and relatively minuscule audience, photography familiarized an often unsuspecting mass audience with the concepts of modernism. This appeal to a wide public was made possible by the perfection of the photo reproduction processes used by newspapers and magazines, leading to a large increase in the number of such publications given over to photography in the service of photojournalism. Fashion magazines also played no small role in the exploitation and dissemination of modernist concepts. This successful melding of artistic, technological and commercial concerns was an intrinsic feature of the American art deco movement – in the design of architecture and architectural interiors, in the design of furniture and household accessories, and in industrial design, as well as in photography.

Invented in 1839 by French artist Louis Daguerre and introduced to the United States through the efforts of telegraph inventor and painter Samuel F B Morse, photography had become a widely employed medium during the latter half of the nineteenth century. Initially used for portraiture, photography was soon being used to document the natural scenic wonders of the American West and the tragic results of the Civil War. By the end of the century, the invention of flexible film to replace the ungainly glass plates had made the medium accessible to hordes of enthusiastic amateurs, the more dedicated of whom sought to prove that photography could equal painting as a serious art form.

Experiments in stop-motion photography conducted in the 1870s and 1880s first by English-born Eadweard Muybridge, and then by Philadelphia painter Thomas Eakins provided important antecedents to twentieth century modernist developments. Muybridge's *Animal Locomotion* studies resulted in the invention of the motion picture. Indeed, films could be regularly seen in all major American and European cities by 1897. And Eakins' human motion studies, based on a technique invented by French physiologist Etienne-Jules Marey, foretold futurist interests in depicting motion and speed, and were a notable prototype for Marcel Duchamp's *Nude Descending a Staircase*.

These motion investigations, conducted in the spirit of scientific inquiry, were balanced by experimentation in photographic technique with more aesthetic ends. Pictorialist photographers experimented to produce works that resembled the atmospheric tonalist paintings being done by James Whistler, George Inness and others, or that approximated the hazy effects of impressionist painters. At the end of the nineteenth century, the pictorialist photographers rejected the ability of photographs to produce images remarkable for their crystalline clarity, and attempted instead to achieve soft romantic effects through the manipulation of development processes and by employing such methods as deliberately taking pictures out of focus or through gauze-covered lenses.

Alfred Stieglitz's 1902 Photo-Secession group, whose membership included Edward Steichen, Clarence H White, Gertrude Käsebier and Alvin Langdon Coburn, had its roots in the pictorialist movement. But exposure to recent develpments in modern European art through Stieglitz's influential avant-garde quarterly, *Camera Work* and by exhibits of modernist art work at Gallery 291 led to a break with the pictorialist tradition. By the middle of the next decade, the Stieglitz group came to promote the view that 'straight,' or unmanipulated photography was the preferable option. This turnabout coincided with the rise of cubism and of the machine aesthetic. The technological miracles of the early twentieth century and the dynamism of its urban environment became a subject of absorbing interest for the futurists, constructivists and precisionists, as well as for avant-garde photographers.

Among the landmark modernist photos were those taken by Boston's Alvin Langdon Coburn. His 1911-1921 views of New York City, taken from above or from other unusual angles, approached abstraction in their compositional effects. And his subsequent vortographs – photographs taken through a kaleidoscope – referred even more closely to cubism's geometric abstraction and fragmentation techniques.

Man Ray's photographs of the 1920s and 1930s also utilized experimental techniques to explore modernist art concerns. His rayographs, or cameraless prints of opaque objects, including machine parts, laid on light sensitive photographic paper, paralleled the widespread modernist interest in machine imagery. The angular purity of machine forms and the rhythmic repetition of geometric shapes were also suggested by the stylized, abstracted patterns of art deco. Similar photograms, as they were more generally known, were also produced by American constructivist sculptor Theodore Roszak, as well as by Laszlo Moholy-Nagy, who was particularly interested in the effect of light variation on photogram images. (Constructivist Moholy-Nagy, who was a Bauhaus teacher in the 1920s, emigrated to Chicago in the 1930s.)

The other modernist American photographers were less technically manipulative than Man Ray. Edward Steichen, who initially began as a painter and a pictorialist photographer, shifted his interest to 'straight'

photography as a result of his assignment as an aerial photographer during World War I, when he had to produce images with the utmost clarity of detail. The results of his aerial work were such a revelation that Steichen systematically began to relearn the fundamentals of photographic technique. From 1923 to 1938, Steichen worked for *Vogue* and *Vanity Fair* magazines as a pioneering fashion photographer and also produced a remarkable series of portraits of celebrities of the 1920s and 1930s. Through the use of brilliant lighting and dramatic dark shadows, he brought the angular diagonals and decorative abstraction of cubism, and of art deco, to many of his sophisticated fashion layouts and to his elegant portraits.

The work of Berenice Abbott underwent a similar metamorphosis, albeit in subject matter. Abbott, who originally went to Europe to study sculpture, became Man Ray's assistant in 1923. This experience led her to take up a photographic career herself. Despite her rapid success as a Parisian portraitist, she returned to America in 1929, drawn by the dynamic developments in New York City and by the possibilities of the metropolis as photographic subject matter. Abbott's mission became to document the physical transformation of New York, preserving on film historical landmarks as well as the process of new construction during the city's skyscraper-building boom. This monumental project was undoubtedly inspired by French photographer Eugene Atget's exhaustive documentation of rapidly disappearing Old Paris and its people. (Abbott personally saved the then virtually unknown Atget's archive for posterity, and was responsible for creating his posthumous reputation.) Abbott worked on her New York photographic project for some ten years. From 1935 on, Abbott's work was aided by the Federal Art Project, and many of these photographs were later published in the book, *Changing New York*. Abbott's New

Below: Thomas Eakins, *Pole Vaulter (George Reynolds)*, 1884.

Above: Man Ray, *Clock Wheels*, 1925, rayograph.

York photographs concentrated on the architectural, machine, and urban imagery preferred by many of the precisionist painters and used by art deco designers. In these photographs she frequently employed unusual and dramatic viewpoints and perspectives, or close-ups, to enhance the abstract, geometric and heroic quality of her subject matter.

Such techniques of abstraction in 'straight' photography were pioneered by Paul Strand in the second decade of the twentieth century. Impressed by the theories of cubism, Strand experimented with geometric abstraction by experimenting with close-ups and by exploiting shadows as compositional elements. He was encouraged in these investigations by Alfred Stieglitz, who devoted the last issues of *Camera Work* in 1917 to Strand's innovative photographs. Strand's 1917 closeup of the inside assembly of an automobile wheel was probably the first photograph to explore the elegant geometry of machine parts. In the early 1920s, Strand completed a series of photographs recording the inner mechanisms of his Akeley film camera. (In 1921, Strand together with Charles Sheeler had made a short film titled *Mannahatta*, that combined dramatic views of New York City with selections from poems by Walt Whitman.) Strand's groundbreaking photographs, based on cubist compositional techniques and promoting the machine aesthetic, energized American art and commercial photography as a whole, and inspired a number of other photographers to explore industrial and urban themes in the context of a cubist vocabulary.

Like Strand, precisionist painter Charles Sheeler was a pioneer in photography informed by cubist conventions.

Sheeler, who took up photography in 1912 to support his activities as a painter, initially documented projects for Philadelphia architects. He soon became interested in exploring on his own the possibilities of Pennsylvania barns as vehicles of structural order. Sheeler had been invited to show six paintings in the Armory show, and the European cubist works in the exhibition had been a profound revelation to him, providing a new direction for his photographic experimentation. His widening reputation brought him a prestigious commission to document the Ford Motor Company Plant at River Rouge, near Detroit, Michigan. By adept selection of camera angles, careful compositional consideration, and effective cropping of these industrial images, Sheeler was able to emphasize the formal and abstract quality of the factory structures. Publication of the River Rouge photographs in the United States, Europe, Japan and even Russia brought Sheeler as well as the monuments of American industry, worldwide recognition and enthusiastic appreciation. The River Rouge plant was also to become a lifelong subject of many of Sheeler's paintings.

Among those photographers influenced by Paul Strand was Paul Outerbridge, who had worked as a stage designer before he became interested in photography as a result of a United States Army assignment in World War I. After study at New York's Clarence H White School of Photography, he began, too, to explore the cubist aesthetic of rhythmic form and structure in architectural and industrial subject matter. Outerbridge's 1923 photograph of a crankshaft summed up the concept that an

Below: Berenice Abbott, *Manhattan Bridge, Looking Up*, circa 1936-40, gelatin silver print.

isolated and gleaming machine part possessed an elegance equivalent to that of a piece of modern abstract sculpture. A fellow student of Outerbridge at the Clarence H White School of Photography was Ralph Steiner, on whom the work of Paul Strand had also made a deep impression. Steiner's freelance work in advertising and magazine illustration similarly drew upon the imagery of the machine and of the geometric complexities of the modern urban scene. His photographs were hailed by, among others, art deco designer Paul Frankl in his 1928 book on furniture and interior design, *New Dimensions*. Steiner was also instrumental in persuading his classmate at the Clarence H White School of Photography, Margaret Bourke-White, to abandon soft-focus pictorialism and to take up unmanipulated straight photography.

Margaret Bourke-White's prolific career, during which she produced over 250,000 photographs, was closely tied to the rise of photojournalism in the 1920s and 1930s. During the nineteenth century, the technology to reproduce photographs in newspapers, magazines and books was virtually unavailable. The historic photographs of the American West and of the Civil War served only as guides for wood engravers. But around 1880, the photo-engraving process was perfected to the extent that half-tones could begin to replace wood engraving illustrations. As the technology improved and editorial prejudices against photographic reproductions waned, by 1900 such newspapers as *The New York Times* and the *Chicago Tribune* were regularly reproducing halftone illustrations. In 1907, regular wire transmission of photographs was initiated between Paris and London, and seven years later, *The New York Times* introduced its rotogravure *Mid-Week Pictorial Review*, which later became the Sunday magazine supplement. By 1919 a number of major newspicture services had been established, among them, the Associated Press, Wide World Photos and International News Photos.

Time magazine, which first appeared in 1923, incorporated photographs, although of a fairly poor reproduction quality, as essential adjuncts to its news stories. But it was *Fortune* magazine, born in the unfortuitous year of 1929, that pioneered photographic journalism in the United States. For its pictorial essays with exquisitely reproduced halftones, *Fortune* hired the foremost European and American photographers. The well-designed unique look of the magazine and of its photographs, many of them of industrial subject matter, earned the title of 'Fortune pictures' for the modernist images on its pages. Concurrently, such progressive fashion magazines as *Vogue* and *Vanity Fair* turned increasingly from illustrations to photographs. In 1936 came *Life* magazine, inspired in part by such popular European prototypes as *Paris Match* and *Berliner Illustrirte Zeitung*. With its full-page photographic reproductions and its dramatic covers, *Life* virtually defined the American photo essay, and attracted a variety of imitators, the longest lived of which was *Look* magazine.

In these developments, Margaret Bourke-White played a central role. She began her professional career in 1927 in Cleveland, Ohio, as an architectural photographer. Her epic interior photographs of Cleveland's Otis Steel

Above: Paul Outerbridge, *Crankshaft*, 1923.

Mill were a technical achievement that brought her to the notice of *Time*'s Henry Luce, who hired her as associate editor and photographer for *Fortune*. Her assignments for *Fortune* permitted Bourke-White to continue her exploration of the aesthetic power of industrial America. Her expertise in this field led to an important 1933 commission to create a series of photomurals for the lobby of the new National Broadcasting Company offices in Rockefeller Center. Probably the largest in the world to date, these photomurals were composed of a series of juxtaposed and greatly enlarged close-ups of technological components used in the broadcasting industry. A number of the individual photos employed Bourke-White's effective compositional technique of showing a number of identical machine parts massed together. The repetition of their abstracted geometric shapes resulted in a patterned rhythm that was both visually decorative and also referred to the syncopated rhythm of the assembly line.

The inclusion of photography which incorporated the imagery of the machine aesthetic in Rockefeller Center, widely acknowledged as a masterpiece of art deco interior design, served to validate photography as an appropriate art deco medium. Edward Steichen was also commissioned to execute a photomural based on the history of aviation for the men's lounge of the now demolished Roxy Theater at Rockefeller Center.

Bourke-White's camera also documented architectural monuments of American art deco design. She recorded the construction of the Chrysler building, in which she subsequently located her own studio, with interior design

Left: Lewis Hine, mechanic at work on the radial motor of an airplane, 1932, from *Men at Work*.

by John Vassos. She also recorded that final showcase of 1920s style deco – the 1933 Chicago Century of Progress exposition, as well as the Empire State building, beginning with the mammoth masonry blocks Bourke-White documented in their Indiana stone quarry.

As the economic depression deepened, Bourke-White and other photographers began to explore individual human concerns; in photographs of the machine aesthetic genre, humanity had been almost totally eliminated. Henry Luce engaged Bourke-White as one of the original four photographers for *Life* magazine, the premier issue of which appeared on 23 November 1936. On the cover was a seemingly typical Bourke-White photograph of the New Deal construction project of Montana's Fort Peck Dam, showing a row of immense, diagonally-receding concrete buttresses. But instead of extolling the power and beauty of the architectural forms, her photo essay inside investigated in a sympathetic way the lives of the construction workers and their families on the isolated western frontier.

This renewed interest in humanity became the primary subject matter of photographers during the later 1930s, as the documentation of the miseries suffered by the victims of economic hard times formed a major output of the New Deal-sponsored photographic projects. But another aspect of this human-centered imagery was the focus on the heroic aspects of the American laborer at work. This imagery tied in with similar depictions of idealized, mythologized laborers on many of the art deco sculptural reliefs and murals that decorated the classical moderne buildings of the New Deal era.

This emphasis was also apparent in Lewis Hine's 1932 book of photographs, *Men at Work*, which showed America's construction workers, mechanics, miners, railroad workers, welders and factory workers employed at their trades. The laborers were seen as in control of their machines and architecture, not dwarfed by them. This heroic interpretation of the American scene optimistically predicted the solution and end to the nation's depression-era woes. In similarly heroic fashion, Hine himself mounted the towering girders and recorded the erection of the Empire State Building. This laudatory attitude was a notable departure for the influential sociologist-photographer, who had previously revealed the exploitation of the underprivileged in his photographic projects on the immigrants arriving at Ellis Island, on the tenements and sweatshops of New York City, and on child labor practices. Those earlier projects were executed in the service of social reform, while the *Men At Work* series marked Hines' understanding of the needs of the depression era for hope in the future.

Similar photographs were produced by others, among them *Life* photographer Andreas Feininger. The images in his *Industrial America* range from the machine aesthetic and the heroic worker to the documentation of the nation's abundant natural resources as seen in such industries as mining, oil, electric power, steel and transportation. And as the United States moved toward World

Above: Margaret Bourke-White's *Loudspeakers in Factory at Camden, N.J.* became a panel of her Rockefeller Center NBC photomural.

War II, such imagery acquired a new propagandistic and morale-raising insistence on American superior might and its eventual victory through the agency of those men and women who manufactured the nation's military arsenal.

During the 1920s and 1930s, many other noted photographers besides those already mentioned took photographs that incorporated the techniques and content of the art deco-related machine aesthetic. Among them were Alfred Stieglitz and Walker Evans, and on the West Coast, Ansel Adams, Immogen Cunningham, Alma Lavensen, Sonia Noskowiak, Peter Stackpole, Willard Van Dyke, Brett Weston and Edward Weston.

The cubist-influenced abstract photography directed at common objects and scenes distinguished itself with unusual camera perspectives, including bird's eye views, worm's eye views, oblique angles and dramatic close-ups. Photographers used contrasting light and shadow to emphasize flattened geometric patterns of line, mass and void. The compositional selection and cropping of views enhanced the rhythmic repetition or opposition of machine parts or of linear structural elements. In content this photography paralleled the ubiquitous art deco imagery of patterned, stylized, dynamic designs; of machine imagery; and in the depression decade, of heroic laborers.

2
ARCHITECTURE

In the United States the art deco style's greatest achievement lay in the area of architecture and architectural ornament. Throughout the country there is a rich heritage of buildings from the 1920s and 1930s with characteristically finely crafted embellishment and often sumptuous interiors. Numbered among these major and minor gems are not just New York City's skyscrapers and Rockefeller Center, but also hundreds of apartment buildings, stores, theaters, churches, schools, banks, civic buildings, bridges and dams across the nation. Even though during these years art deco coexisted with various historical revival styles, as well as with the nascent International Style, its wide use and diverse manifestations characterize it as the most popular new style.

Despite art deco's self-conscious modernism and its European affiliations, there were also indigenous American antecedents for its rich ornamentation, color effects and dramatic massing. Two great originals of American architecture, Frank Furness and Louis Sullivan, designed buildings that had much in common with art deco. Furness was Sullivan's teacher, and Sullivan in turn was Frank Lloyd Wright's master. Frank Lloyd Wright, of course, designed several monuments of art deco architecture.

Philadelphia's Furness had studied in the New York atelier of Richard Morris Hunt, and was influenced, as were many other nineteenth-century architects, by the ideas of John Ruskin, who held that beauty in architecture was dependent on decoration and surface effects, particularly as seen in the polychromy of Italian gothic. Ruskin also promoted boldness in massing and ornament derived from nature. In a series of uniquely individualistic commissions – among them, the Pennsylvania Academy of Fine Arts and various Philadelphia banks – Furness put these principles into practice. His remarkable 1879 Provident Life & Trust Company incorporated

eclectic and exotic stylistic motifs, a rich mixture of materials and color effects, and powerful massing. His ornament was indeed based on nature, but was abstracted according to the idea of British designer and writer Owen Jones, who stressed that 'all ornament should be based upon a geometrical construction.'

Louis Sullivan, who is considered one of the few American practitioners of art nouveau, posited an organic approach to building in which form was to follow function, and in which the architecture had to fulfill not only technological and utilitarian ends, but also social and expressive ones. The theories, writings and buildings of Sullivan had a profound impact on the development of American architecture, of the skyscraper and on the uses of architectural ornament. His use of patterned floral

Left: Raymond Hood, McGraw-Hill Building, 1931. Horizontally emphasized with streamlined entrance, it looked to the future.

Right: Frank Furness, Provident Life and Trust Company, Philadelphia, 1879.

Left: John B Peterkin, Airlines Building, New York City, 1939-40.
Above: Fellheimer & Wagner, New York Central Terminal, Buffalo,
New York, 1927-29.

ornament in cast iron and colored terra cotta to emphasize the various parts of a building, and his use of vertical piers interjected with recessed ornamented spandrels later became essential features of art deco design.

Some of Sullivan's ideas could be traced to the theories of nineteenth-century Germany architect Gottfried Semper, whose essay, 'Development of Architectural

Below: George Winkler, Public Service Company Office, Tulsa,
Oklahoma, 1923.

Above: Ely Jacques Kahn, Film Center Building, New York City, 1928-29, facade detail.

Style,' had been translated and published by Chicago architect John Wellborn Root. Semper proposed an evolutionary interpretation of architectural history in which the primary features of primitive housing – the ground floor, the roof, the hearth and the walls of hanging tapestries or animal skins – were to be symbolically stressed in contemporary architecture by ornamental embellishment. Thus the entryways of buildings and their rooflines were to be ornamented, as were their 'curtain walls' with patterns resembling woven textiles. Sullivan's work generally followed these concepts, as did the subsequent art deco skyscrapers with their ornamented entrances, luxurious elevator lobbies and decorated pinnacles. This humanistic use of ornament made the buildings visually appealing to the public at street level as well as from a distance.

Zigzag Moderne

The zigzag-style skyscrapers, the ultimate achievement of American art deco, were completed during a relatively short urban building boom, from about 1925 to 1931, by a number of Beaux Arts-trained architects for a variety of commercial clients. European ideas from the 1925 Paris exposition of decorative arts, from the Wiener Werkstätte, and from German expressionist architecture and theatrical set design influenced the form and ornament of these buildings, as did the primitivism of pre-Columbian architecture and the imagery of the machine age. There was an eclectic recombination and stylization of the diverse motifs to achieve a look that was not just aggressively modernistic, but also symbolically futuristic.

The actual shape the skyscraper took in the late 1920s was determined by two earlier developments. The first was a 1916 New York City zoning ordinance that mandated building setbacks, to be determined by the width of the street. This kind of stepped-back contour resembled a ziggurat topped by a soaring tower. The second decisive event was the 1922 international architectural competition to design a new building for the Chicago Tribune newspaper company. The winning design by Americans John Mead Howells and Raymond Hood was for a conservative gothicized skyscraper complete with flying buttresses at the summit. Chosen from the 263 international submissions, this design reflected the then current trend of skyscrapers in gothic and classical styles. But it was the design that won second place, by Finnish architect Eliel Saarinen, that attracted the most interest. Though also gothic in conception, the Saarinen design liberated the skyscraper from strict reliance on historical styles and suggested instead the way of a modernistic simplification that adapted and combined a variety of decorative motifs. In 1923, Saarinen traveled to the United States to accept his prize and decided to remain. Beginning in 1926, he designed the buildings and other facilities for Cranbrook Academy near Detroit, Michigan, and went on to produce

Above: Ely Jacques Kahn, Film Center Building, lobby and elevator door detail.

Above: Sloan & Robertson, Chanin Building, New York City, 1927-28, facade detail.

some of American art deco's finest furniture and household accessories.

A good deal of credit for popularizing the skyscraper style also was owed to Hugh Ferriss, whose romantically abstracted and visionary renderings of art deco buildings were persuasive in selling new design concepts to clients, as well as generally influencing public acceptance of modernistic architectural trends. Trained as an architect, Ferriss never had any actual buildings constructed after his own design.

Construction began in 1923 on New York City's pioneering zigzag style building, the New York Telephone Building, also known as the Barclay-Vesey Building, designed by Ralph T Walker. Work did not begin on the city's second such structure until 1926. This, the Insurance Center Building, was designed by Ely Jacques Kahn, who had an architectural degree from Columbia University and also had studied at the École des Beaux Arts (as had Raymond Hood and William Van Alen). One of the most talented and productive of Manhattan's art deco architects, Kahn designed over 30 such commercial structures before 1931, including such outstanding examples as the Park Avenue Building, the Film Center Building, the Squibb building and the Casino Building. The first true skyscraper in the zigzag style was Sloan and Robertson's luxurious Chanin Building, commenced in

1927. The archetypal art deco skyscraper was William Van Alen's flamboyant Chrysler Building, with an ornamental frieze of automobile hub caps and mud guards, and accenting winged radiator caps at the base of its fantastic soaring spire. The Empire State Building, topped with a machine age dirigible mooring mast, ended the heroic era of the art deco skyscraper.

Raymond Hood, who was also considered an influential art deco designer despite his relatively small output of four such buildings – including the American Radiator Building, the Daily News Building and the McGraw Hill Building — collaborated with a large group of architects on the design of Rockefeller Center, now considered by many as the greatest achievement of American art deco. The popular and accessible complex of office buildings, theaters, restaurants, shops, and an exterior pedestrian mall was not as important for its monolithic towers as for its success as a planning concept; and for its exterior ornamental sculpture by such artists as Lee Lawrie, Paul Manship, Isamu Noguchi, Hildreth Meiere, Gaston Lachaise, Leo Friedlander, and Carl Milles – as well as for its rich interior design, particularly of Radio City Music Hall by Donald Deskey.

Wealth of surface ornament on the building exterior, and echoed in its interior, was characteristic of the art deco style. Crisply patterned geometric motifs included

Left: Irwin Chanin Office, Century and Majestic Buildings, New York City.
Right: New York City's Empire State Building was topped with a distinctive art deco machine age mast for mooring dirigibles.

zigzags, triangles, stripes, segmented circles and spirals; while among the stylized naturalistic ornaments were flowers, trees, fronds, fountains, gazelles, birds, clouds and sunrises. Astrological imagery, along with idealized personifications of natural and technological forces, was also popular. Expressive of the machine age and its dynamism were lightning bolts, airplanes, locomotives, ocean liners, automobiles, skyscrapers and bridges. The machine-age imagery also extended to the building summits which frequently were mounted with futuristic masts or finned parapets (as were the Century and Majestic buildings by the Irwin Chanin office). Full of aspiration and optimism, the art deco imagery depicted man's place in the cosmos and his confident control of the machine, which would bring the dawn of a new era, a much-longed for earthly paradise.

Often done in striking color, the art deco ornament was executed in a rich variety of media, including terracotta, cast plaster, tile, mosaic, metal, etched or stained glass, stencil, paint, and exotic contrasting wood veneers. Theatrically illuminated, the exquisitely crafted tapestry-like wall ornamentation was part of a total coordinated interior design — which extended to the light fixtures, grilles, stair railings, elevator doors, carpets, furniture,

Below: Bley & Lyman, as consultants to King & King, Niagara Hudson Building, Syracuse, 1932; sculpture by Clayton Frye.

and even mailboxes — cooperatively realized by collaborating architects, designers, artists and craftspeople.

Zigzag art deco was not just a New York City phenomenon; buildings in this style soon were erected nationwide. Some of the more important examples of these structures were commissioned by utility companies. A significant one was Niagara Mohawk's office building in Syracuse, New York. Conceived as a temple of electricity, the building's facade incorporated bands of glass panels covering helium tubes and incandescent bulbs in a dramatic nighttime illumination system. A colossal stainless steel sculpture of the winged *Spirit of Light* was mounted 80 feet above the entrance.

Important groups of zigzag and other art deco buildings were erected in Pittsburgh, Pennsylvania and elsewhere, but one of the most remarkable enclaves of art deco architecture was assembled in the oil boom town of Tulsa,

Oklahoma, during the 1920s and 1930s. Outstanding among the various commercial and civic structures in this style were the buildings of Bruce Goff. Like Barry Byrne and Frank Lloyd Wright, who also designed Tulsa buildings in those years, the individualistic Goff defied categorization. With no formal professional education, Goff learned his craft through apprenticeship. He designed a series of impressive structures – among them the Tulsa Club, the Page Warehouse, the Guaranty Laundry, and the Midwest Equitable Meter Company – which owed a debt to German expressionism. His 1929 Riverside Studio was typically atypical. The boxy white stucco studio, with a gigantic porthole window of decoratively etched glass framed by stepped panels of black glass representing 'musical notation,' had an elegant terrazzo and chromium fountain by Alfonso Iannelli, daringly abstract art deco murals by Olinka Hrdy, and aluminum ceilings.

But it was Goff's dynamic Boston Avenue Methodist Church that earned the widest recognition, with its stylized sculpture, geometric ornament, and cubist-inspired stained glass, suggested by ideas from Claude Bragdon's *Projective Ornament* and *Architecture and Democracy*. Books were essential to Goff's informal architectural education, just as they were a means for spreading the latest modernist architectural ideas, with little time lag, to culturally isolated areas.

During the 1920s, Frank Lloyd Wright completed a number of innovative commissions closely allied to zigzag art deco. Executed in poured concrete and geometrically patterned textile block – a technique pioneered in Wright's 1904 Unity Church and his 1915 AD German Warehouse — these Aztec or Mayan style California residences included the Barnsdall (Hollyhock) house, the Millard residence, the Storer residence, the Freeman residence and the monumental Ennis residence. Wright's oldest son, Lloyd Wright, an architect as well, supervised the construction of these houses, and went on himself to design other California buildings inspired by pre-Columbian forms. Frank Lloyd Wright also worked on several major commercial projects with affinities to art deco. Predated by the surprising 1903 Larkin building, these were the Midway Gardens pleasure palace adorned with Iannelli's stylized sculptures, Tokyo's Imperial Hotel whose floating foundation allowed it to survive the disastrous 1923 earthquake, and the Arizona Biltmore Hotel with Aztec motifs designed by sculptor Emry Kopta.

Southern California, which underwent a period of remarkable growth and prosperity during the 1920s, was

Below: William Van Alen, Chrysler Building, 1930.

Below: Bruce Goff, Boston Avenue Methodist Church, Tulsa.

Above: F L Wright, Barnsdall House, Los Angeles, 1917-20.　　**Below:** F L Wright, Barnsdall (Hollyhock) House, interior.

the site of a number of exotic variations on zigzag deco, as well as of related revival styles. The Aztec style was also seen in Robert Stacy Judd's flamboyant Monrovia Aztec Hotel, and in Morgan, Walls and Clements' Mayan Theater in Los Angeles. Bertram Goodhue adapted Egyptian ornament for his Los Angeles Public Library, and Assyrian decorative motifs were adapted for the Samson Tyre and Rubber Company, later the Uniroyal Tire Factory, by Morgan, Walls and Clements, who also produced such other zigzag art deco treasures as the black and gold Atlantic Richfield Building, the Dominguez-Wilshire Building, the Security Pacific Bank building, the Warner Brothers Western Theater/Pellissier Building, and the Leimert Theater, now a Jehovah's Witness Hall.

The sculptural relief motifs seen in New York City's skyscrapers were also utilized by West Coast designers, sometimes in an exaggerated form that marked the predilection of Californians for strikingly dramatic effects, and underlined the general art deco tendency to treat stage-set-like entrances of buildings in a luxuriously theatrical way. The characteristic ornamentation of the entrance facades that was continued into the lobby area highlighted the emphasis on public accessibility of the commercially-oriented zigzag style.

Right: F L Wright, Arizona Biltmore, Phoenix, 1927.
Below: Robert Stacy Judd, Aztec Hotel, Monrovia, Calif., 1925.
Far right: Arizona Biltmore lobby.
Far right below: Morgan, Walls & Clements, Samson Tyre, 1929.

Classical Moderne

Although zigzag moderne architecture was aptly expressive of the commercially-minded, forward-moving, flamboyant 1920s, it was not an appropriate style for all clients. In fact, many preferred historical revival styles in the buildings they commissioned. But there were also those clients, often governmental or civic, who preferred a dignified modernistic architecture of a more conservative nature. This kind of art deco architecture, which combined simplified classical forms with a rather more austere exterior and interior decoration, has been variously called 'classical moderne,' 'neoclassical moderne,' 'international stripped classicism,' 'PWA (Public Works Administration) art deco,' or 'PWA moderne.' To simplify matters, henceforth this style shall be referred to as classical moderne.

Because the great depression, beginning with the 1929 stock market crash, dealt a catastrophic blow to most new commercial building projects and because the government, under the aegis of Franklin D Roosevelt's New Deal programs, stepped in to alleviate the ever-widening unemployment through a program of federally sponsored construction projects, the classical moderne style – which was often the architectural style of choice – came to be associated closely with the New Deal's Public Works

Administration and the Works Progress Administration (WPA). During the 1930s, hundreds of post offices, libraries, schools, city halls, courthouses, museums and other civic structures in the classical moderne style were erected nationwide, thus making classical moderne the mostly widely represented of the art deco architectural styles in the United States.

Training in the classical precepts of architecture, in the Beaux Arts tradition, remained central to the education of professional architects during the early decades of the twentieth century. In the years between the two world wars, both European and American architects began to experiment with the abstraction, or simplification, of classical building types. Josef Hoffmann was in the forefront of this movement in Vienna, as were Peter Behrens in Berlin and Edwin Lutyens in Great Britain. Among the first American architects, around 1910, to attempt to modernize classical forms was Bertram Goodhue (1869-1924). Goodhue, who had apprenticed with the renowned gothic revival architect James Renwick and had worked for some 23 years with yet another gothic revivalist, Ralph Adams Cram, demonstrated his growing interest in modernism with his simplified 1910 West Point Chapel. But it was Goodhue's bold 1916-1928 design for the Nebraska State Capitol in Lincoln that fundamentally established the prototype for governmental construction in the classical moderne style.

The Nebraska State Capitol building was an innovative amalgam of modernistic and classical, of skyscraper and

Left: Morgan, Walls & Clements, Pellissier Building/Wiltern Theater, Los Angeles, 1930-31, lobby.
Below: Gilbert S Underwood, Omaha Union Station in Nebraska.

temple, with a stable simplified mass, an arched entrance, and a dramatic soaring golden domed tower. Goodhue's design, which won the 1920 competition, was tied also to concurrent work by modernist architects in the Scandinavian and Germanic countries (and hence was an appropriate choice for Nebraska, where so many immigrants from Northern Europe had settled). Like Eliel Saarinen's Helsinki station, the Nebraska Capitol exterior incorporated stylized stone carvings and low reliefs (by Lee Lawrie). This ornamentation was restricted to the four entrances, thus emphasizing the plain smoothness of the rest of the flat wall surfaces. Goodhue personally supervised the artistic program of the building, choosing not only sculptor Lawrie, but also Augustus Vincent Tack to design murals and Hildreth Meiere to execute colorful mosaic ornamentation for the interior vaults. Following Goodhue's death – reportedly hastened by aggravations associated with the Nebraska project – the work on the illustrative murals, mosaics and friezes adorning the ceremonial interiors went on for another 40 years.

The architectural decoration of art deco buildings during the 1920s and 1930s provided substantial careers for a number of specialized sculptors and painters. Lee Lawrie, who was best known for his heroic *Atlas* at Rockefeller Center, designed stylized classically-inspired sculpture for various other important buildings, including Goodhue's Los Angeles Public Library. Also a sculpture consultant for the 1933 Chicago and 1939 New York world's fairs, the German-born Lawrie apprenticed with Augustus Saint-Gaudens and received a degree from Yale University, where he executed architectural sculpture for the Harkness Memorial Quadrangle.

Hildreth Meiere, who had studied at the Beaux-Arts Institute of Design, was one of the few women to become commercially successful in this field. A past president of the National Society of Mural Painters and a winner of a 1928 Architectural League award, she was elected to the National Academy of Design. Meiere's official commissions included architectural decoration at Rockefeller Center, the New York World's Fair, and for the ocean liner *United States*.

The towered Louisiana State Capitol at Baton Rouge, completed in 1933, was directly inspired by Goodhue's impressive Nebraska design. Built to the specifications of the state's demagogic governor, Huey Long, by the New Orleans architectural firm of Weiss, Dreyfous and

Below: Bertram Goodhue, Nebraska State Capitol, Lincoln, 1922-32, north entrance.

Below: Gilbert S Underwood, Omaha Union Station lobby, 1929-1930.

Seiferth, the capitol building's extensive illustrative and symbolic ornament included carvings by Lee Lawrie and Lorado Taft, with murals and painted geometric ornament by Jules Guerin, Louis Borgo and Andrew Mackey. Among the subjects portrayed were Louisiana colonial era history, Civil War battles and Mardi Gras revelry. The regional imagery extended even to the column capitals — which depicted carved turtles and alligators. The building's luxurious interiors were done in an art deco style resembling a chic night club. Following Governor Long's 1935 assassination in the capitol's halls, the building became a monument to his memory.

After viewing the Baton Rouge capitol and that of Nebraska, the North Dakota capitol commission decided that they too wanted a towered building to replace the old Bismarck capitol which had burned down in 1930. The Chicago architectural firm of Holabird and Root provided a rather austere complex with a tower off to one side. And in 1935 the Oregon state capitol burned down, and New York architect Francis Keally's design won the competition for the new structure. The new building had a flat-topped central cylindrical tower, symmetrical

Below: Dreyfous & Seiferth, Louisiana State Capitol, Baton Rouge, 1933. The extensive sculptural program included Lorado Taft's *The Pioneers* on the building's west buttress (*left*).

massing, and simplified wall surfaces relieved by flat vertical piers. The Oregon capitol, which was partially paid for by PWA funds, also included a historically oriented art program of sculpture by Leo Friedlander, and murals by Barry Faulkner and F H Schwartz.

Many of the city halls built in the classical moderne style during the 1930s followed the example of the state capitols. For them, too, elaborate and symbolic artistic programs were considered appropriate and necessary complements. Notable among these city halls were that of Los Angeles designed by John C Austin, Albert C Martin and John Parkinson with a tower like that of Goodhue's Nebraska capitol; Buffalo City Hall designed by Dietel

Left: Griffith Observatory, Los Angeles, designed in 1934 by John C Austin and Frederick M Ashley.
Below: Department of Water Power Building, Lincoln Heights, LA.

and Wade, Sullivan W Jones; Holabird and Root's St Paul City Hall and Ramsey Courthouse; Wight and Wight's Kansas City Hall; Nashville, Tennessee's City Hall, originally designed as a courthouse by Frederick C Hirons and Emmons H Woolwine; Houston City Hall by Joseph Finger; and Oklahoma City's Municipal Building by Allied Architects.

These uses of the classical moderne style in the state capitols and city halls erected during the 1930s generally were characterized by classically balanced masses, with an emphasis on symmetry and horizontality, except for the towers, which looked back to the skyscraper style. The exterior columns customary to historical classical styles were replaced by flattened piers, which sometimes were fluted but usually lacked capitals or bases. The monumentality of these buildings was enhanced by flat, simplified wall surfaces, usually executed in stone, granite, marble or terrazzo. Relief and freestanding sculpture frequently adorned the exterior, although to a more limited degree than in the zigzag style; usually the entrance areas were embellished while the other wall surfaces remained unadorned. At times the classical moderne interiors were surprisingly flamboyant, with a profusion of murals, relief sculpture, mosaics, ornate metalwork, uniquely attractive lighting fixtures, and with the walls and paneling executed in a variety of interesting materials – including marble and exotic, often contrasting, wood veneers. The imagery of the artwork was usually symbolic of the function of the building, or of its community and local history. Optimistic portrayals of stylized heroic workers in local agricultural or industrial activities represented, as did the dignified permanence of the architecture itself, the local civic and national aspirations of continuity, stability and perseverance through hard work. During the troubled economic and social climate of the 1930s, such allusions were particularly reassuring and encouraging.

In stylistic terms, the classical moderne architectural style represented, at least to some degree, a compromise between the highly ornate and vertical zigzag style, and the relatively austere and horizontal streamlined style characterized by aerodynamic form. Classical moderne was, too, a compromise between modernity and traditionalism.

Paul Philippe Cret (1876-1945) was a leader among those classical moderne architects who adhered more closely to classical principles of design, while still accommodating modernism. Cret, who was born in France and educated at the Ecole des Beaux Arts, moved in 1903 to the United States, where he taught at the University of Pennsylvania until 1937. Among his most important architectural commissions, many of them completed in collaboration with other architects, were the 1922 Detroit Institute of Arts, the 1929 Philadelphia Rodin Museum, the 1932 Folger Shakespeare Library in Washington, DC, his dramatic Hall of Science at the 1933 Chicago Century of Progress exposition, and the 1937 Federal Reserve Building, also in Washington.

When his firm was hired to tackle problems of interior design, Cret became much more ornate in his use of art deco detailing. A prime example was Cincinnati's Union

Terminal, designed by Roland Anthony Wank of Fellheimer and Wagner in 1933. Brought in as a consultant to the railroad, Cret was responsible for enriching the original conservative classicist design with such modernist accoutrements as mosaic murals and a glittering rotunda ceiling by Winold Reiss, decorative murals by Pierre Bourdelle, a tearoom decorated with Rookwood tiles, specially designed aluminum and leather furniture, exquisite metalwork door guards and ventilator grilles, and elegantly streamlined elevator interiors, designed by Cret himself. In his continuing work for the railroad, from 1933 to 1945, Cret's firm designed the interiors of 64 different railroad cars for Philadelphia's Edward G Budd Company.

The diversity of applications of the classical moderne style can be seen in Tulsa, Oklahoma, which, as noted earlier, had a sumptuous heritage of zigzag deco buildings that had been built at the height of its oil boom. Despite the general austerity engendered by the depression, Tulsa's structures in the classical moderne style were frequently enlivened by colorful ornament. Notable was the 1932 Fairgrounds Pavilion designed by architect Leland I Shumway. The sedate balanced forms of the structure contrasted with the polychromatic terracotta tile and low relief friezes above the entrances and at the roof line – incorporating bovine heads, horses and other imagery alluding to the agricultural function of the pavilion.

Above: Fellheimer & Wagner, Cincinnati Union Station, 1929-33. This art deco monument has since been demolished. *[handwritten: 1993 Its still there]*
Below: Leland I Shumway, Fairgrounds Pavilion, Tulsa, Oklahoma, 1932, detail of sculptural ornament.

And Tulsa's 1938 Will Rogers High School, designed by Arthur M Atkinson, Leon B Senter and Joseph R Koberling Jr, was featured at the time of its dedication in *Time* magazine as a praiseworthy high school of the future. The school, on which construction had begun in late 1937, was one of the first PWA projects in the state of Oklahoma. Its dignified, symmetrically massed forms were accompanied by art deco detail remarkable in a public educational structure. The entrance, which was surmounted by relief sculpture in floral motifs framing octagonal portraits of Will Rogers above exquisitely worked metal spandrels, led to a main hall of terracotta sheathed walls, terrazzo floors, and ornamental plaster work borders by sculptor Percy Prosser. The classrooms were originally painted pastel colors that had been scientifically proven to facilitate the learning of specific subjects. And the balconied school auditorium resembled an ornate art deco theater – with brass fan-shaped insets, gold leaf, red floral designs, elegantly constructed lighting fixtures, and a mural by Chicago interior decorator Alex Rindskopf. Of course most of the schools and other civic buildings constructed under the auspices of the New Deal programs did not equal the Tulsa high school in splendor.

But stylized ornament did remain an important feature of classical moderne architecture. Many of the zigzag style motifs continued in use, along with some additions. The eagle, also a symbol of the New Deal's National Recovery Administration (NRA), came to be frequently seen, as were the stylized depictions of heroic workers in classicized relief panels and murals. The eagle as a nationalistic symbol and the glorification of workers and industry reflected the social and political exigencies of the depression years.

Streamlined Moderne

The third architectural manifestation of the art deco style was known as streamlined moderne. A style of aerodynamic curves, horizontal orientation, flat roofs, glass brick and banded windows, steel railings, speed stripes and mechanistically smooth wall surfaces, the streamlined style in architecture paralleled that used by the industrial designers of airplanes, locomotives, automobiles and household appliances. Streamlining's optimistic and futuristic implications of machine-like efficiency and active movement forward continued the symbolic program initiated by the zigzag style.

First predicted in the German expressionist architecture of Eric Mendelsohn and others, and in the futurist drawings of Italian visionary architect Antonio Sant'Elia, streamlined architecture initially appeared on the American scene in two key transitional buildings. Raymond Hood followed his earlier Chicago Tribune, American Radiator, and Daily News buildings with the 1931 McGraw Hill building, a zigzag style skyscraper placed on a colorful horizontally banded base curving in to enclose a streamlined lobby. And William Lescaze's and George Howe's design for the 1932 Philadelphia Savings Fund Society building mounted a functionalist International Style office tower on a streamlined base with a curved facade of glass and polished charcoal granite.

Below: Robert Derran, Coca Cola Bottling Plant, Los Angeles; remodeling began in 1937.

Lescaze, who was also an active designer of furniture and interiors, later transformed a nineteenth-century Victorian townhouse by means of glass brick and streamlined sheathing, into a thoroughly modern New York City residence.

In its fully developed version, the streamlined style became a popular choice for numerous substantial commercial buildings nationwide. California, the site of an extensive building boom during the 1920s and 1930s, boasted many notable examples, including the Winnie and Sutch Company building in Huntington Park, and the Los Angeles Coca Cola Bottling Plant by Robert Derran.

Now widely acknowledged as the masterpiece of the streamlined style, the Johnson Wax complex in Racine, Wisconsin, was Frank Lloyd Wright's largest corporate commission. Here the disciplined curves of the exterior were echoed in the luminous banded ceiling of the reception area and the monumental columns of the clerical hall. Wright's decorative use of glass tubing for innovative lighting effects, his coordinating curvilinear office furniture, and sleekly finished exterior walls expressed the machine aesthetic and modern corporate efficiency. Wright's investigations of curved forms culminated in his 1943 design for the Guggenheim Museum, which was finally erected in the late 1950s. The streamlined architectural style, with all its futuristic resonances, climaxed at the end of the decade in the 1939 New York World's Fair.

Above: Streamlined diners became a feature of the landscape.

The streamlined style was never widely favored for domestic housing, although there were a limited number of such curvilinear, flat-roofed, horizontal and white stucco residences commissioned by self-consciously avant-garde and financially well-off clients, particularly in California, on the East Coast and also in Tulsa, Oklahoma. A notable example was the Des Moines, Iowa, house built by Kraetsch and Kraetsch for owner Earl Butler, who collaborated on the design of the tornado, earthquake, fire and termite-proof structure which incorporated such radical features as electric eye-controlled garage doors and an intercommunicating telephone system.

The streamlined style was far more appreciated by commercial clients. Not only was it used for a whole range of new, modest, sometimes prefabricated roadside structures such as gas stations, diners, bus terminals and stores, but it was also heavily utilized in the context of the 'modernize Main Street' movement, beginning in 1936, to renovate countless traditionally styled commercial structures by applying modernistic facades of such machine-age materials as vitrolite (baked enamel panels), black glass, aluminum and plastic, along with neon tube lighting. Not only the streamlined, but also the zigzag style was expressed in such relatively inexpensive image transformations that sought to attract new customers.

Eventually the streamlined style became accepted as a well-established commercial style and as such was the architecture of choice for a number of business structures throughout the 1940s and later.

A more regional and exotic variation of art deco architecture was the 1920s Pueblo revival style inspired by the American Indian structures of earlier centuries. Sometimes referred to as Pueblo deco, residential houses built in this style generally featured thick adobe-like walls, flat roofs masked behind curved or stepped parapets, crisply geometric surface articulation, rows of projecting vigas (rustic log rafters), and stylized corbels (support members). Such structures were popular in the American Southwest.

That in art deco architecture stylistic lines were continually crisscrossed was demonstrated by the offshoot of streamlined moderne known as tropical deco. Tropical deco is named for its Florida locale but similar buildings were constructed in southern California and elsewhere. The concentration of tropical deco architecture – some 400 buildings – in the square mile of the historic district now known as Old Miami Beach was the result of an intensive southern Florida building boom that ran from the late 1920s through the 1930s.

Designed by such relatively little known architects as Albert Anis, L Murray Dixon, Roy F France, Henry Hohauser, Anton Skislewicz, and B Robert Swartburg, Miami's tropical deco hotels, apartment buildings and

houses confirm the basically vernacular nature of art deco architecture — not only in the frequent anonymity of tropical deco's designers, but also in its idiosyncratic quality.

Generally constructed inexpensively of concrete covered with stucco, the tropical deco buildings tempered the aerodynamic, horizontal, speed-striped efficiency of the streamlined style with zigzag style setbacks, polychromy, and stylized organic and abstract ornament. The functionalist white of streamlined wall surfaces was frequently painted over with such sensuous pastel hues as flamingo pink, sea green and yellow. And when the curved walls of streamlining were supplanted by the cubist boxiness of the International Style, their austere linearity was softened by the curves of the applied ornament. And frequently the horizontal structures were topped with futuristic machine age masts, previously seen on New York's zigzag skyscrapers. Sometimes these masts were finned, or served to display jazzy neon signs.

The distinctive features of tropical deco included cantilevered sunshades over windows, octagonal and porthole windows, flag staff parapets, and deck-like balconies. The latter features were part of the site-specific marine imagery of tropical deco, as were such regional ornamental motifs as dolphins, herons, mermaids, seashells, alligators, flamingos, palm trees, and stylized waves and clouds. Special meaning was imparted to the popular sunburst and fountain motifs — Florida, the sun wor-

Above: Frank Lloyd Wright, Guggenheim Museum, New York City, designed in 1943 but not erected until the late 1950s.
Below: The tropical deco of Miami Beach evoked an exotic fantasy.

Above: F L Wright, Johnson Wax Building, Racine, Wisc., 1936-39.
Left: McCarter & Nairne, Marine Building, Vancouver, 1929-30.

shipper's mecca, was after all the site of Ponce de Leon's fabled fountain of youth. The opulent, seductive quality of the interior and exterior ornament helped to reinforce the fantasy of a glamorous Hollywood-style vacation paradise, a welcome escape from the mundane problems of daily life.

Art deco architecture also gained a foothold elsewhere on the North American continent. In Mexico, during the height of its post revolutionary artistic renaissance of the 1920s and 1930s, a series of splendid schools, hospitals, office buildings and apartment buildings were designed by Juan O'Gorman, José Villagran Garcia, Enrico de la Mora and other architects.

To the north, Canadian cities also possessed a rich heritage of art deco architecture. On the West Coast, Vancouver's most magnificent example was McCarter and Nairne's Marine Building. The city's tallest structure for many decades, the zigzag style office building was encrusted with modernistic polychromatic ornament. The building's terra cotta panels illustrated the discovery of the Pacific Coast and depicted the history of transportation. Vancouver's City Hall by Townley and Mathewson

Above: Adrian Gilbert Scott, St James Church, Vancouver, 1935-37.
Right: Ernest Barott, Bank of Montreal, Ottawa, 1930-34.

was built in a stepped back classical moderne style, with applied geometric ornament on green spandrels between the windows and with decorative friezes. One of the city's more unique monuments was St James Anglican Church by Adrian Gilbert Scott, an angular modernistic adaptation of gothic revival. And in the dominion's capital of Ottawa, the classical moderne Bank of Montreal headquarters by Ernest I Barott was embellished with decorative metalwork and Emil Sieburn's elegant relief sculpture, which allegorically depicted aspects of Canadian industry and commerce.

In Montreal, the residence known as Maison Cormier – a sophisticated amalgam of art deco ornament and the International Style – was later classified as a national historic monument. Ernest Cormier, an outstanding Quebecois architect, was also designer for the University of Montreal. But many of Canada's art deco treasures – in the form of office buildings, apartment buildings, department stores and movie theaters – unfortunately were demolished in the decades following World War II. An interest in preserving such unique architectural monuments developed only fairly recently.

3
FURNITURE
AND INTERIOR DESIGN

The primary impetus for American art deco furniture design came from Europe through the means of imported pieces and of imported talent. As a number of important European designers – among them, Joseph Urban, Kem Weber, Paul Frankl, Walter von Nessen, William Lescaze, Ilonka Karasz, Wolfgang and Pola Hoffmann, and Eliel Saarinen – began to move to the United States around the time of World War I, they became leaders in a movement that eventually transformed the fashionable domestic and commercial interior environment, bringing it in line with the concepts of modernism and of the machine aesthetic. At the same time, most of the American-born designers – among them Donald Deskey, Gilbert Rohde, Eugene Schoen, Ruth Reeves, Raymond Hood and Ely Jacques Kahn – either studied or traveled in Europe, gaining firsthand knowledge of the latest developments in modern design. It is also significant that many of the furniture and interior designers were architects or originally had studied architecture.

During the early twentieth century, the most inventive American furniture designers were those of the Arts and Crafts Movement. Although they sought a break with traditional forms of furniture by designing simple and attractive pieces that were appropriate to their environment, the emphasis of these craftspeople on high-quality handwork severely limited their output. The art deco designers sought to reconcile these goals of superior design and quality with the modernistic style and production capabilities of the machine age. The stylistic inspiration for American art deco furniture came primarily from Austria and France. The innovative modernist designs produced by Josef Hoffmann, the leading spirit of the Wiener Werkstätte, were particularly influential – around 1910, he already made stepped, or ziggurat-shaped case furniture. The Viennese ideas were brought to the United States by Joseph Urban (in 1911), Paul Frankl (in 1914) and other Austrian immigrants.

The 1925 Paris exposition of decorative arts also had a decisive influence. The United States had been invited to participate but secretary of commerce Herbert Hoover declined on the grounds that Americans could not meet the exposition requirement of 'original' design. The modernist luxury furniture of leading French designers was a revelation to the thousands of Americans and the 108 members of the official US commission who attended the exposition. A selection of works from the Paris exposition also traveled in 1926 to the Metropolitan Museum of Art and to eight other American museums. The elegant one-of-a-kind French pieces were characterized by simplified flat surfaces enriched with

Left: F L Wright's *Tree of Life* window for his 1904 Martin House in Buffalo was an important forerunner of art deco design.
Right: Such Arts and Crafts objects immediately preceded art deco.

Above: Ralph Walker, Man's Study for 1929 exhibit, *The Architect and the Industrial Arts*, Metropolitan Museum of Art.

decorative veneers of contrasting exotic woods, gleaming lacquers, and inlays of ivory, mother of pearl and other unusual materials. In opulence and workmanship they equaled the masterpieces of eighteenth-century French cabinet makers. Stylistically also the French furniture possessed a strong affinity to neoclassicism.

Below: Mahogany and aluminum desk, circa 1930.

The Austrian and French designs were made available to the American audience through specialized shops and galleries. One of the earliest was the Austrian Workshop, opened in New York in 1919 by Rena Rosenthal, the sister of Ely Jacques Kahn. In the 1920s major department stores such as Macy's, Lord & Taylor, Wanamakers, B Altman, and Abraham & Straus began to host exhibits of modern design. Public interest was intense as in the first week alone some 100,000 people visited the 1928 Macy's 'First International Exposition of Art in Industry,' which included both European and American work shown in zigzag style display cases designed by Lee Simonson.

Following the example of the pioneering Newark Museum, other American museums began to hold displays of design works. The most important exhibits were those staged by the Metropolitan Museum of Art in an attempt to foster collaboration between designers and industry. The Metropolitan's 1929 'The Architect and the Industrial Arts' exhibit featuring 13 room ensembles designed by leading architects – among them Ely Jacques Kahn, Ralph Walker, Joseph Urban, Eugene Schoen, John Wellborn Root, Eliel Saarinen and Raymond Hood – was so popular that its length had to be extended from six weeks to six months. The versatile architects designed not only the integrated modernistic furniture and accessories, but also the textiles and decorative geometric wall treatments. As was typical of the 1920s style, most items of furniture were costly unique pieces. Some critics justifiably complained that the designs were inaccessible to all but the wealthy few. Root was perhaps the exception in that he later put his women's bedroom furniture into production and had it sold through Montgomery Ward outlets.

Toward the end of the decade, many French designers began to refuse to participate in American exhibitions because of the unethical practice of some department stores, among them Lord & Taylor and Macy's, of making unauthorized reproductions of their furniture. An exception was the French architect-designer Lucien Rollin who visited New York in 1934 to mass produce his finely crafted wood furniture in collaboration with W & J Sloane department stores at a cost that made it widely available.

The stylistic sources of 1920s American art deco furniture included the neoclassical and empire styles (in the refined use of contrasting veneers, of octagon and oval motifs, of fluting, and of pedestal bases), Chinese furniture (in the low center of gravity and the use of black and colored lacquers), the machine aesthetic (in the use of such new materials as chromium, aluminum, and bakelite), cubism (in the volumetric and angular shapes, and the use of bright colors and geometric ornament), and primitivism (in the use of exotic woods and unusual natural materials). The inventive combination of these traditional and modernist motifs in a decorative way distinguished art deco from the other more austere modernist styles.

One of the finest American furniture designers of the 1920s was Eugene Schoen, who had a 1901 architecture degree from Columbia University. After the 1925 Paris exposition, Schoen established an interior design firm and

Above: Console table with mirror, probably by Dan Cooper, ca. 1930.

Above: Eugene Schoen, mahogany cabinet.

a New York gallery selling his own and imported designs. In his varied commissions for luxury apartments, bank interiors, theaters and department stores, Schoen exploited the decorative possibilities of contrasting wood veneers, of lacquered orientalism and of dignified neoclassical proportions. His most important commission of the following decade was the interior design of the RKO Theater at Rockefeller Center. Schoen's pieces ranged from the conservatively moderne to the modernistic exploration of such machine age materials as glass and metal.

The most distinctive motif of 1920s American art deco furniture was the skyscraper style so forcefully promoted by Paul Frankl in his articles and books on the modern design movement. Frankl created desks, desk-bookcases and dressing tables in the stepped skyscraper style, often in exotic wood veneers or highly polished light-toned

woods enhanced with vividly hued lacquers or even gold and silver leaf. Frankl believed that the furniture inside a modern urban apartment should harmonize with the metropolitan skyline seen through its windows. He also produced more conservative neoclassically inspired pieces such as a chrome-mounted center table for New York's Metropolitan Life Building. As did the other designers, Frankl also designed smaller household accessories such as a Telechron brass and bakelite mantel clock, with a decorative sunburst of rays of silver and gray – an art deco motif related to the neoclassical fan motif.

The skyscraper style was also taken up by other designers, among them Abel Faidy, who designed a luxurious skyscraper style suite for a Chicago penthouse. A Swiss-born architect, Faidy also designed commercial interiors and created furniture designs for Chicago manufacturers. Another memorable Chicago art deco ensemble

was the ebonized and pewter inlaid dining room suite designed by Hal Pereira for a wealthy client. Pereira later moved to California where he became a Hollywood set designer.

The important New York art deco architect Ely Jacques Kahn, who was much in demand because of his flexible attitude toward modern design, also executed many interior design commissions that required the design of specialized furniture. An unusual example was Kahn's glass, marble and chromed metal luminaire/planter. The design of new types of combination furniture was characteristic of the art deco era. The more cramped quarters of the fashionable skyscraper apartments called for furniture adaptable to many functions, and the social life of the jazz age also called for new types of furniture, such as bar consoles and cocktail tables – with bakelite tops resistant to spilled alcohol and cigarette burns. Even such traditional furniture types as wicker armchairs were redesigned by Frankl, Donald Deskey, Gilbert Rohde and others in dramatically angular shapes accommodating compartments for drinks and magazine racks. The incorporation of electric light fixtures into furniture was another art deco phenomenon. Kem Weber, for example, designed a skyscraper style dressing table with vertical light tubes flanking the mirror.

Joseph Urban, whose most important architectural designs were New York's Ziegfeld Theater and the New School for Social Research, and who worked as a theatrical designer for the Metropolitan Opera and the Ziegfeld Follies, also designed furniture. Inspired by Wiener Werkstätte ideas, Urban's furniture was sold through the New York outlet of the Viennese design workshop, of which he was the American manager.

Art deco ideas also spread quickly beyond the urban centers, as seen in the unique modernist furniture handmade by Wharton Esherick, a painter, sculptor, graphic artist and woodworker who practiced his craft in the relative seclusion of Paoli, Pennsylvania. Through his work as an avant-garde stage designer during the 1920s, Esherick became familiar with German expressionist stage sets. Hence, his 1929 victrola cabinet, designed as a sculptural/functional base for the carved wooden statue of a stylized dancer, reflected expressionist as well as art deco ideas in its accentuated triangles, and oblique geometric and organic surface articulation achieved through directionally opposed wood grains.

Probably the greatest accomplishment of art deco furniture were the sophisticated designs created by Eliel Saarinen. Shortly after his arrival in the United States, Saarinen became involved in the establishment, together with newspaper publisher George Booth, and construction of Cranbrook Academy of Art outside Detroit, Michigan. As chief architect, interior designer and furniture designer for the academy's buildings, Saarinen created a remarkable integrated setting for a unique combined artistic community and educational institution that nurtured and trained, under his directorship, a

Left: Eliel & Loja Saarinen, designers, and Loja Saarinen & Walborg Nordquist Smalley, weavers, *Rug No. 2*, 1928-29, cotton warp, wool pile.

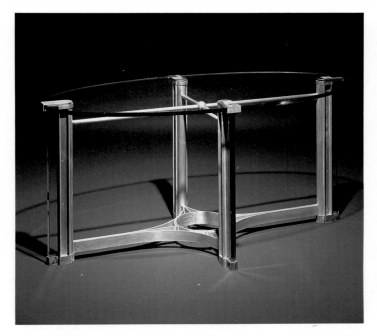

Top: Eugene Schoen, nickel and glass center table, circa 1932, designed for Rockefeller Center.
Above: Abel Faidy, dining table of veneered maple, 1927.
Right: Abel Faidy, skyscraper style armchair, 1927.

generation of innovative designers, artists and crafts-people. Among Saarinen's most elegant designs were the furniture made for his own residence at Cranbrook. Restrained zigzag geometric motifs embellished in veneer the surfaces of the living room chairs, cabinets and tables constructed in a combination of exotic woods. The dining room chairs, with graceful linear fluting, surrounded a circular table exquisitely inlaid in a radiating geometric pattern. Originally, the dining room's octagonal shape, octagonally patterned rug, custom designed light fixture, textiles, paneled walls and even the dishes (designed by Saarinen to match the chairs) harmonized with the furniture. This kind of total design of rooms and of public spaces was characteristic of art deco. Elements from the

Saarinen residence – notably the tiled living room fire-place and the octagonally patterned rug – were also displayed as part of Saarinen's dining room ensemble at the 1929 Metropolitan Museum exhibition. The exhibited chairs, however, were of a different design that subtly echoed the skyscraper style.

The economic depression brought radical changes to the design and production of art deco furniture. There was, in effect, a repudiation of the luxurious style of the 1920s and a new focus on less costly mass produced items. Materials such as plastics, metals and variations on glass that had once been used in art deco furniture to represent the machine aesthetic and modernism now became essential materials for affordable furniture. This move toward

Above: Paul Frankl, silver lacquered desk, with trapezoidal top above frieze drawer with silver-plated pulls, circa 1930.
Below: Paul Frankl, writing desk, zebra wood and lacquer, circa 1930.

Above: Eliel Saarinen, round table and side chairs, on octagonal rug, 1929-30, among the items originally designed for architect's residence at Cranbrook.

Above: Ely Jacques Kahn, luminaire/planter.
Above right: Wharton Esherick, *Finale* on victrola cabinet, 1929.
Right: Joseph Urban, table, black lacquer, silver trim, circa 1920.

a functionalist aesthetic also was encouraged by the emphasis given to ideas emanating from the Bauhaus by way of American industrial design exhibits of the late 1920s and by the new Museum of Modern Art's vigorous espousal of International Style and Bauhaus design concepts. And when the Nazis closed the Bauhaus in 1933, this brought a second wave of influential European functionalist designers to the United States. The functionalist art deco furniture of the 1930s meshed with the streamlined style promulgated by the rising generation of American industrial designers.

Nowhere was the change more apparent than in the 1934 Metropolitan Museum exhibition, 'Contemporary American Industrial Art,' in which the architect-designed room now embraced the new aesthetic. The chairs, tables, and even a Steinway piano were mounted on metal legs or bases, glass brick window walls were introduced, and Saarinen even produced a lady's room with blocky built-in furniture embellished with horizontal speed stripes. During the depression decade a number of furniture designers – Donald Deskey, Gilbert Rohde, and Kem Weber among them – carved out successful careers by creating functionalist art deco designs to be mass produced by hitherto traditionally oriented furniture manufacturers. Often the manufacturers turned to modernist designs from sheer economic desperation and some, notably the Herman Miller company, even thrived as a result.

One of the most successful designers of the era was Donald Deskey, who originally had studied architecture and painting in the United States and Paris. While in Europe, he visited the Bauhaus and also was impressed by Dutch De Stijl design. In 1927 he established the design firm of Deskey-Vollmer together with Phillip Vollmer.

What differentiated Deskey's furniture designs from the more austere functionalism of the Bauhaus was a respect for ornament and comfort, and an eclectic regard for historicism. Thus, for example, his side chair was designed with double steel banded legs when single bands would have been structurally adequate, and the seat and back were thickly upholstered. And Deskey's chrome and black glass table on U-shaped supports – a characteristic art deco feature also used by leading French designers – was, despite its modernistic materials, majestically reminiscent of the empire style. As were many other art deco designers, Deskey was also influenced by contemporary developments in avant-garde art; he adapted the stylization of cubism, for example, in the hand-painted screens he executed during the 1920s for Paul Frankl's gallery and on commission for individual clients. A notable example was the lacquered wood and chrome screen he created for drama critic Gilbert Seldes, who wrote an adaptation of Aristophanes' play, *Lysistrata*.

Left: Eliel Saarinen, side chair for architect's residence at Cranbrook, 1929-30.
Below: Eliel Saarinen, round table for architect's residence at Cranbrook, 1929-30.
Opposite left: Donald Deskey, upholstered and steel side chair.
Opposite right: Donald Deskey, chromed metal and black lacquer desk lamp.
Opposite below: Donald Deskey, chrome and black glass table.

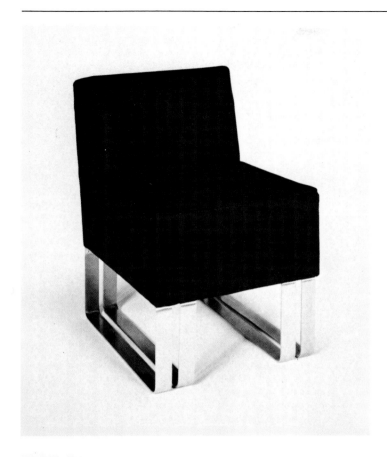

Diversity was a quality that also marked Gilbert Rohde's career. As an industrial designer, Rohde concentrated on the creation of progressive furniture designs utilizing new materials and new manufacturing techniques. Among Rohde's noted mass produced designs were laminated and bentwood chairs inspired by Finnish architect Alvar Aalto's designs, and sectional sofas. Stylistically, Rohde ranged from 1920s deco veneered furniture to functionalist pieces of plastic and tubular steel. His 1935 desk/bookcase for the Herman Miller company was reminiscent of the exotic veneering of the opulent 1920s style, but the design was characteristically innovative in its space saving (only 17 inches deep) and multifunctional concept. For less traditional tastes he designed a bakelite topped and square tubular metal framed desk that was advertised as the ultimate in modern functionalism, not only in its clean geometric lines, but also for its 'no mar,' 'no tarnish' surfaces. The desk's color combination of silvery metal and black bakelite,

Left: Joseph Urban, Man's Den for 1929 exhibit, *The Architect and the Industrial Arts*, Metropolitan Museum of Art.
Right: Donald Deskey, Dining Room for 1934 exhibit, *Contemporary American Industrial Arts*, Metropolitan Museum of Art.
Below: Eliel Saarinen, Room for a Lady for 1934 exhibit, *Contemporary American Industrial Arts*, Metropolitan Museum of Art.

Above: Alvar Aalto, # 400 lounge chair, late 1930s.
Below: Russel Wright, Modern Living furniture line, 1935.

glass or lacquered wood was a popular one in art deco design. Rohde also dreamed up such inventive interior settings as walls banded in alternating horizontal strips of brushed copper and cork. His modernist designs for the 1933 Chicago exposition's 'Design for Living' house brought him widespread recognition.

Equally successful was the German-born California-based Kem Weber, who had been stranded in the United States by the outbreak of World War I. His varied activities included industrial design, interior design and Hollywood film set design, as well as the design of individually commissioned and mass produced art deco furniture ranging from the ornately decorative to comfortably upholstered metal tubular chairs.

For the 1932 'Machine Art' exhibition at the Philadelphia Art Museum, Russel Wright was commissioned to build a modernistic breakfast room with all the furniture, accessories and even the window blinds fabricated of aluminum, which was considered a wonder metal at the time. But such machine age furniture was not popularly appreciated in the domestic context, and Wright subsequently became less enamored of new materials and production techniques, and more interested in the humanistic and functional possibilities of wood. His

Above: F L Wright, desk and chair for Johnson Wax Building, 1936-39, walnut, Cherokee Red enamelled steel, brass plate.

sturdily made and reasonably priced *Modern Living* furniture line of solid maple was unusual in that most wooden art deco furniture sheathed cheaper structural wood with elegant veneers of most costly woods. The line was produced in a reddish tone, as well as in an unstained 'blond.' The blond look, which was also favored by Aalto, became a desirable feature of art deco furniture in general. Wright's furniture, which looked traditional but also was modern in its rectilinearity and rounded edges, became an almost immediate best-seller after its festive 1935 introduction at Macy's. And Wright further democratized modern design in that the *Modern Living* line could be purchased as a total room unit – including harmonizing textiles, accessories and lamps. Up to now, the option of a totally designed room had been available only to the wealthy who could afford such custom work.

Certainly the most insistent proponent of the totally designed environment was Frank Lloyd Wright. From the time of his pioneering Prairie houses, he had designed individualistic, freestanding and built-in furniture to complement the architectural surroundings. While Wright's earlier furniture designs resembled the work produced by the artisans of the Arts and Crafts movement, those of the 1920s and 1930s reflected art deco ideas. The chairs that he made for the exotic Tokyo Imperial Hotel were allied, in their geometric vitality, to the zigzag style. A later resonance of the zigzag style occurred in the 1937 office interior Wright designed for Edgar Kauffman's Pittsburgh, Pennsylvania, department store. Here the elegant geometrically patterned wall paneling harmonized with the cubist style furniture; both were a matching light toned natural finish. Wright's important commercial projects also provided him with furniture design opportunities. For the 1903 Larkin building he designed some of the earliest metal office furniture, introduced vertical steel filing cabinets, and

attached legless steel chairs to the desks to make office cleaning easier. With the Johnson Wax company project of the 1930s, Wright returned to the problem of office furniture, designing desks and chairs in curved and streamlined forms that reflected the architecture. Although visually sophisticated and artistically inventive, Wright's chair designs generally were insensitive to the needs of their users; they were notoriously uncomfortable. An early critic compared them to a 'fiendish instrument of torture,' and Wright himself later admitted that he had become 'black and blue' from sitting on them.

Frank Lloyd Wright also personally designed lamps, rugs and stained glass for his buildings. He disliked curtains so he often used geometrically patterned stained glass windows as screens in his Prairie houses, in Midway

Below: F L Wright, Johnson Wax Building. Most of the original furniture has now been removed or modified.

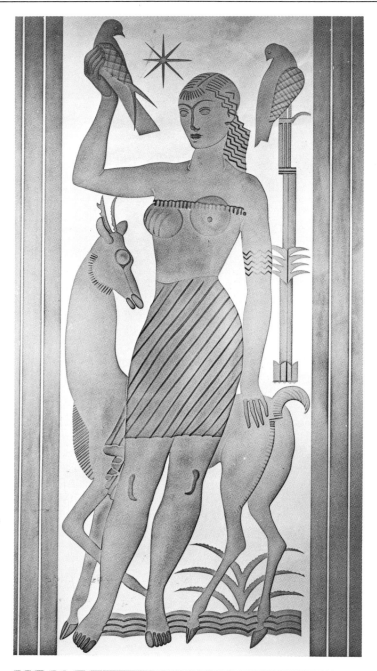

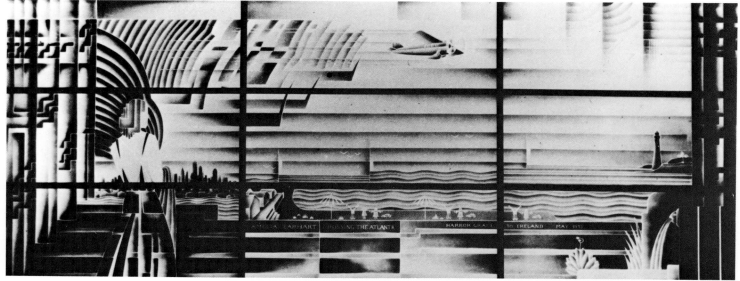

Gardens, in the Barnsdall house and in other projects. This pointed the way for other architects and soon art glass manufacturers met the demand by producing stained glass with geometric or stylized floral patterns. Stained glass remained a popular architectural embellishment throughout the art deco years in residential and commercial settings, not only for windows but also for doors, partitions, door lights and skylights. Among the more favored decorative motifs were geometric patterns, zodiacs and stylized elements from nature, including plants, waves, clouds and sunrises.

A speciality of the art deco years was clear glass etched, sandblasted, painted, or embossed with geometric or stylized representational imagery. Characteristic were the panels designed by Edgar Miller for the clerestory of Chicago's Diana Court. Their classically derived imagery was similar to that of Sidney Waugh's Steuben glass designs, and to art deco architectural sculpture. The versatile Miller designed stained glass, made sculpture and executed murals for various churches, restaurants and clubs. Also striking were the glass murals made by Maurice Heaton for interiors designed by Eugene Schoen. Heaton's illuminated *Amelia Earhart* mural for Rockefeller Center's RKO Theater was the most impressive of these works. (Heaton also made handcrafted modernistic art glass items that were sold in Schoen's and Rena Rosenthal's galleries.) Glass was used decoratively in interior design in other ways as well. Textured glass, glass block, geometrically leaded clear glass, cut or painted black glass, blue glass and mirrors were used to create dramatic effects. The widespread interest in architectural ornamental glass was an integral part of the persistent art deco fascination with theatrical lighting effects.

As architectural elements and as necessary domestic accessories, electric light fixtures were also inventively interpreted. Frank Lloyd Wright and Alfonso Iannelli designed modernistic lighting fixtures, as did many other important art deco designers. Those created by Donald Deskey varied in type from a rectilinear glass box on a fluted base to a hemispherical cubist-inspired desk lamp allied to Bauhaus ideas. One of the most typical art deco lights was the torchere, a freestanding columnar lamp that provided indirect illumination by aiming the machine age shade at the ceiling. The art deco torchere was a reinterpretation of a classical style lighting standard. Walter von Nessen created probably one of the most elegant versions of the torchere although many others – among them Russel Wright and Eliel Saarinen – designed torcheres. Nessen, who initially supplied architects with lighting fixtures and metal furnishings, expanded his design studio during the 1930s to sell functionalist furnishings to retailers. In architecturally installed lighting, the fixtures translated the diverse motifs of art deco, from

Opposite above: Edgar Miller, etched glass panels depicting the goddess Diana, 1929-31, from the clerestory of Diana Court in Holabird & Root's Michigan Square Building, Chicago.
Opposite below: Maurice Heaton, *Amelia Earhart Crossing the Atlantic*, glass mural for RKO Roxy Theatre, Rockefeller Center.
Right: Walter Von Nessen, standing floor lamp, brushed chrome over brass, iron base, circa 1928.

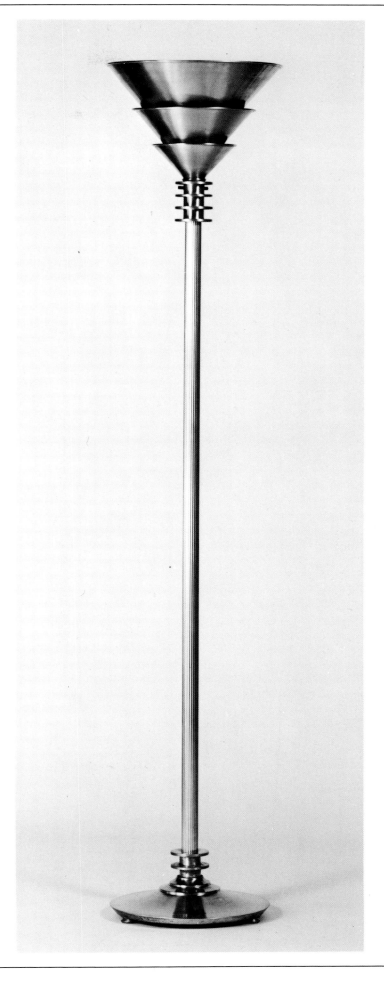

Above left and right: Walter Kantack, pair of chromed bronze masks for RKO Roxy Theatre, Rockefeller Center, circa 1932.
Left: W Wyatt Hibbs, designer, cast aluminum elevator doors, US Port Office & Court House, Norfolk, Virginia, circa 1932.
Right: Maja Andersson Wirde, designer, and Studio Loja Saarinen, weavers, *Animal Carpet*, 1932, linen warp, wool weft.

the geometric to the stylized figurative, as demonstrated by the chromed bronze masks created by lighting specialist Walter Kantack for the RKO Theater. Decorative animal motifs were used by W Hunt Diederich for a more old-fashioned light fixture, the chandelier.

Skilful metalwork was required to produce such fixtures and was also employed in the creation of other interior accessories. Diederich designed as well firescreens embellished with graceful silhouetted greyhounds. Eliel Saarinen, too, was involved in the design of decorative metalwork, not only for the gates to Cranbrook Academy, but also of the elegant peacock andirons for the fireplace of his residence there. French-born designer Jules Bouy, who headed Ferrobrandt, Inc – the New York outlet for the prominent French art deco ironworker Edgar Brandt – designed such items as an ornate wrought iron mantelpiece. Among the other accessories sold by Ferrobrandt were lamps, firescreens, andirons, tables and mirror frames – all ornamented with graceful art deco motifs.

Important decorative components of the coordinated art deco interior were textiles and carpets. Characteristic of the multidisciplinary activity of the artists and designers of the era were the textile and rug designs created by Ely Jacques Kahn, photographer Edward Steichen, photographer and precisionist painter Charles Sheeler and sculptor John Storrs. The leading textile designers were Henriette Reiss, Ilonka Karasz and particularly Ruth Reeves. Reeves, who had studied at New York's Pratt Institute and the Art Students League, spent most of the 1920s in France where she studied with Fernand Leger. Her handblocked textile and rug designs reflected the cubist ideas of Picasso and Leger. In 1930, W & J Sloane commissioned her to create 29 designs that ranged in content from rhythmic geometric abstraction to stylized representational imagery evoking the American urban and social life of the era.

Handworked and embroidered textiles and wall hangings were also created for interiors. Among the more important interpreters of stylized art deco imagery in this medium were Marguerite Zorach, Mariska Karasz – sometimes in collaboration with her sister Ilonka – Lydia Bush-Brown and Arthur Crisp. Such art deco motifs occasionally extended even to the folk art hooked rugs worked by anonymous makers far from the fashionable urban circles of design.

Room-sized and wall-to-wall carpets for domestic and public interiors were in demand. Chinese art deco rugs were imported, renewed appreciation developed for Navaho rugs, and designers frequently created unique patterns for special settings, as at Rockefeller Center, or for Oakland's Paramount Theater. Again, some of the most sophisticated art deco carpets and textiles were those made at Cranbrook Academy. Eliel Saarinen's wife Loja Saarinen headed a workshop that produced a series of remarkable carpets and textiles, primarily for Cranbrook and for the nearby Kingswood school. Most were designed by Loja Saarinen, at times in collaboration with her husband, or by accomplished resident weavers such as Sweden's Maja Andersson in art deco geometric, zigzag,

skyscraper, animal and other motifs in a way that subtly harmonized with their interior settings.

The dramatic quality of art deco environments was distinctively seductive. Department stores had recognized the style's power of attraction early on by hiring the likes of John Vassos, Norman Bel Geddes, Louis Lozowick, Frederick Kiesler, Donald Deskey and even Alexander Archipenko to create striking window displays. Designers were also commissioned to invent alluring modernistic interiors for airplanes, trains and ocean liners. Restaurants, night clubs and hotels additionally kept leading art deco designers and architects busy. Ely Jacques Kahn transformed the interiors of the Broadmoor Restaurant and Rutley's Restaurant with stylized cloud murals on the ceilings and walls. John Mead Howells created an art deco aura for the tower lounge of New York's Panhellenic Building. Winold Reiss designed the interiors of the Crillon Restaurant, the Congo Room at the Hotel Almac, and in later years the Indian Room of Montreal's Chic-n-Coop Restaurant. Other designers dreamed up exotic and elegantly primitivistic settings for Harlem's all white nightclubs. Even such sedate institutions as banks judged it essential to remain in fashion – Hildreth Meiere's red and gold mosaics enveloped the main banking room of New York's Irving Trust Building.

Below: Kem Weber, Mayfair Hotel, Los Angeles, 1926-27.

Above: Van Nest Polglase, art director, *Top Hat*, 1935. Hollywood set designers also used art deco ideas.
Right: Timothy Pflueger, Paramount Theater, Oakland, Calif., 1931.

In Los Angeles, Kem Weber executed an opulent zigzag style interior for the Mayfair Hotel. The best known art deco environment, of course, was that created for Rockefeller Center, particularly the coordinated interior design of Radio City Music Hall by Donald Deskey where the machine age aesthetic of streamlining was juxtaposed with the luxurious stylized nature imagery of the earlier zigzag style. Another remarkable theater was Timothy Pflueger's Oakland Paramount – a magnificent combination movie-vaudeville palace that was an extravagant fantasy of zigzag style pattern, imagery and light.

The Hollywood films and vaudeville stage productions also offered the Depression-era masses settings of vicarious luxury. Art directors provided such films as *Top Hat* and Ernst Lubitsch's sophisticated romantic comedies with elegant art deco decor. A particular Hollywood specialty, both in films and in movie star's homes, was the 'white look,' which photographed so effectively in black and white films.

The more ephemeral settings of vaudeville dance extravaganzas also reflected the modernistic stylization of art deco. A recently uncovered archive of scenic renderings by Anthony Nelle, a Polish-born ballet dancer (and one time partner of Anna Pavlova), choreographer and production designer who created stage sets for New York's Roxy Theater and for the Fox theaters in Detroit, St Louis and San Francisco showed such typical art deco devices as oblique diagonals, ray lines, soaring skyscrapers and streamlined transportation motifs. The popular entertainments of film and vaudeville provided a welcome, if temporary, escape from the cares of the Depression era.

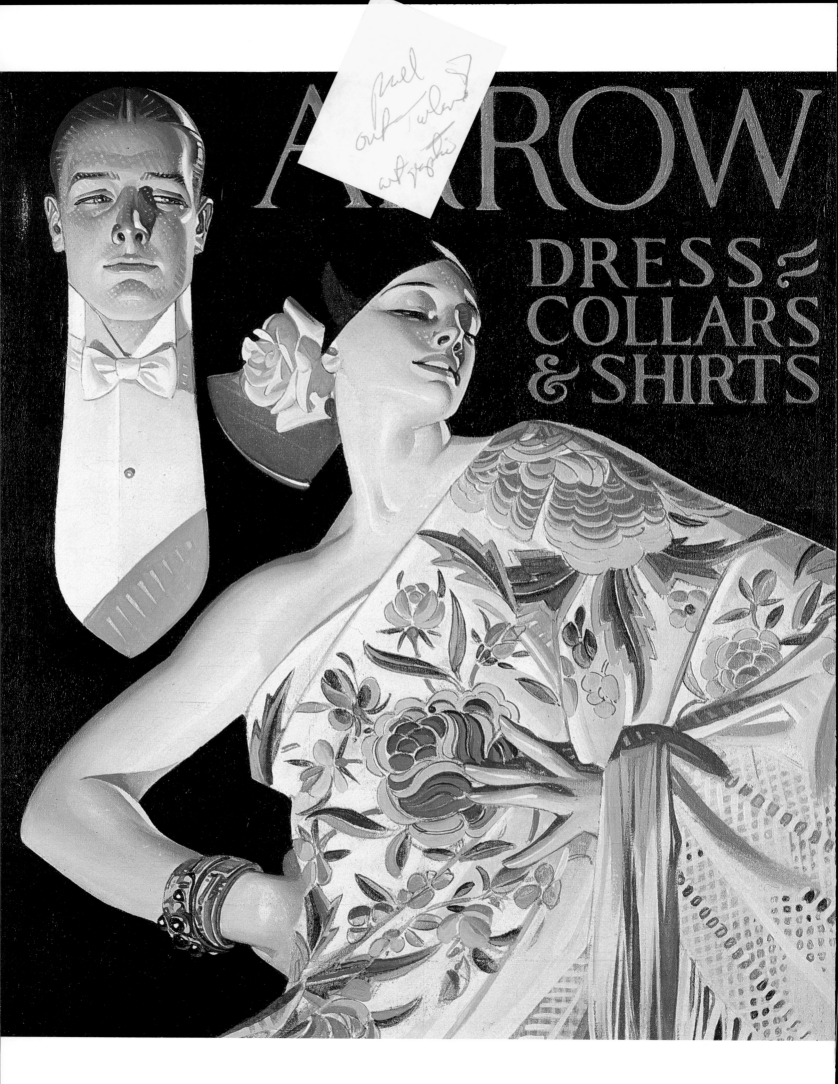

4
ILLUSTRATION
AND GRAPHIC ART

The conventions of art deco were also rapidly assimilated by those artists who produced images for books, magazines and posters. Again, the diluted influence of cubism was apparent, to a greater or lesser degree, as were aspects of other modernist art movements. And as was true in the field of furniture and household accessories design, a number of the important artists executing illustrations or graphic designs were either European immigrants or were European-trained. The lure of American opportunity was a strong one in the 1920s, and in the following decade the rise of fascism drove many important European designers to seek refuge in the United States. There were also a number of Americans who sought and found a greater cosmopolitanism and artistic success in Europe. To an even greater degree than with photography, illustrations and posters were a medium through which the motifs of art deco were disseminated to a mass audience.

Probably the most elite form of illustration was that done for books. During the 1920s and 1930s, there was great interest in the production and collection of limited edition illustrated, well-designed and finely-printed books. Frequently the high production cost of illustrated books was offset by the practice of first issuing deluxe, high-priced volumes in signed, limited editions, later followed by low-cost editions that sold widely to the general public. Another profitable strategy was to produce concurrently with the mass edition, 'special copies' of a book that incorporated such features important to collectors as expensive bindings, supplemental plates and wider margins.

Of the book illustrators of the art deco era, the most prolific and best known was Rockwell Kent, who originally studied architecture at Columbia University and worked for a time as an architectural renderer before he turned to painting. Kent's career as an illustrator began

in 1914 with the publication of a series of drawings by *Vanity Fair*. He continued to produce elegant and satirical drawings of fashionable and foolish members of New York society for other publications as well, among them *Harpers Weekly* and *Puck*; and he numbered Rolls Royce among his advertising clients. Kent also tried his hand at designing ceramic ware, silverware, jewelry and

Left: J C Leyendecker, illustration for Arrow Collar advertisement, circa 1922.
Right: J Floyd Yewell, *New York Central Terminal, Buffalo, New York*, 1929 (Fellheimer & Wagner, architects).

textiles. But his most successful venture was in the field of book illustration, and in many cases the uniquely high quality of the books he illustrated was due in no small part to Kent's total involvement in all details of the book design. He was also overwhelmed with commissions to design book plates, book jackets and bookmarks.

Kent had a markedly romantic side that led him on sporadic travels to such remote regions as Alaska, Newfoundland, Greenland and Tierra del Fuego. He recorded these travels and published them as illustrated books – among them, *Wilderness: A Journal of Quiet Adventure in Alaska* (1920), *Voyaging Southward from the Strait of Magellan* (1924), *N by E* (1930), and *Salamina* (1935). These books of personal adventures were as eagerly received as Kent's illustrated versions of Voltaire's *Candide* (1928), Melville's *Moby Dick* (1930), Chaucer's *Canterbury Tales* (1930), *Beowulf* (1932), Butler's *Erewhon* (1934), Shakespeare's *Complete Works* (1936), *Paul Bunyan* (1941) and Goethe's *Faust* (1941).

Kent's ink and crayon illustrations characteristically resembled wood engravings, a craft he also practiced. Such drawings reproduced especially well, with their dramatic contrasts of light and dark, and of void and mass. The effect of deeply receding planes achieved through the use of parallel horizontal lines and the idealized monolithic human figures and topography suggested epic events and primeval mysteries of man and nature. The architectonic quality of many of these illustrations not only recalled Kent's own architectural education, but also had an affinity to the quasi-mystical skyscraper renderings of Hugh Ferriss. In Kent's illustrations, the simplified elongated human figures; the rhythmic repetition of lines, angles and curves; the sharp contours, and the sculptural relief-like effect closely reflected the decorative motifs of art deco architectural surface designs and relief sculpture.

Many other artists were attracted by the boldly stylized black and white illustration style used by Rockwell Kent. Among them were Paul Landacre, Henry Glintencamp, William Wolfson and James Reid. The style was also used to dramatic effect by Canadian artists – foremost among them Bertram Booker in his 1930 illustrations to Dostoevsky's *Crime and Punishment*, and his 1933 drawings for *The Ancient Mariner*. During his northern travels, Rockwell Kent had come in close contact with a number of artists of the Canadian Group of Seven. Their stylized northern landscapes and those of Rockwell Kent had so much in common that it is difficult to judge just who influenced whom.

In the United States, another prolific illustrator producing works in a high contrast black and white art deco style was Lynd Ward, whose most remarkable works were his textless novels in woodcuts – *God's Man, Vertigo, Mad Man's Drum*, and *Song Without Words*. Ward's 1929 *God's Man*, a Faustian tale of a modern artist, incorporated images of soaring skyscrapers and jagged

Left and right: Rockwell Kent, illustrations for *Wilderness: A Journal of Quiet Adventure in Alaska*, 1920. From the top the titles are 'Home Building,' 'Unknown Waters,' 'Get Up,' and *right*, 'Zarathustra Himself Led the Ugliest Man by the Hand. . . .'

Left: Bertram Brooker, 'Realization,' from *Crime and Punishment*.
Above left and right: Hugh Ferriss' dramatic architectural renderings
helped to popularize the art deco style.

mountains seen from dramatic and oblique angles. Among
Ward's other important commissions were his illustrations for Oscar Wilde's *The Ballad of Reading Gaol*
(1928), Goethe's *Faust* (1930), Richard Wagner's *The
Story of Siegfried* (1931), Mary Shelley's *Frankenstein*
(1934), Homer's *Odysseus* (1934) and Donald Culross
Peattie's *A Book of Hours* (1937). As were many illustrators of the era, Ward was versatile in his choice of technique and style. Besides the black and white woodcuts, he
also did elegant stylized line illustrations in conservative
art deco style; and later in the 1930s and 1940s he produced line and colored illustrations in the more realistic
regionalist style used by Thomas Hart Benton and John
Stuart Curry. During these years, Lynd Ward also
illustrated a number of children's books.

With the influx of modernist ideas, the 1920s and 1930s
were a time of intense activity and development in
American children's book illustration. Even a number of
textbooks produced during these years were strikingly
illustrated. According to some authorities, the strength of
children's book art in the United States lay in the area of
black and white illustration, while British children's
books were known for their pastel colored pictures, and
the forte of French children's books was their boldly
colored illustrations. No doubt, this classification over-
simplifies the matter, as American publishers certainly
could produce effective color illustrations. Notable were

those done by Mary Lott Seaman for the *Golden Goose*, in
which art deco concerns were reflected in the flat areas of
vivid arbitrary colors, the stylized absence of three-
dimensionality, and the studied effect of parallel or
diagonal planes. The very active Maud and Miska
Petersham's illustrations for *The Poppy Seed Cakes*
(1924) incorporated similarly bold colors, suggested
perhaps by the exotic set and costume designs for the
Ballets Russes, along with decorative stylized friezes
around the text pages. The folk art quality of *The Poppy
Seed Cakes* echoed similar interests of such art deco
designers as Winold Reiss and W Hunt Diederich.
Stylized illustrations in a softer, more volumetric form,
some in black and white and some in color, were done for
American children's books by Helen Sewell and by Ingri
and Edgar Parin D'Aulaire.

But strikingly high contrast black and white stylized
pictures, reflecting art deco interests, were often the
choice of many prominent children's book illustrators,
among them Virginia Lee Burton, Russian emigre Boris
Artzybasheff and Wanda Ga'g. Ga'g's 1928 classic,
Millions of Cats, also possessed a folk quality, and the
high contrast black and white illustrations recall the fact
that Ga'g produced frieze decorations for the *New
Masses*, where some of the most important graphic work
of these years was published. The coarse porous news-
print of the periodical required bold images that reproduced well, and Ga'g used a similar style for her children's
book illustrations.

Illustrated books by architects also served to explicate
and disseminate art deco ideas. Notable were the simple

Above: John Vassos, 'Dromophobia, the Fear of Crossing the Street,' and 'Acrophobia, the Fear of High Places,' from *Phobia*, 1931.

stylized line drawings done by architect Claude Bragdon for *Projective Ornament* (1913) and his personal manifesto, *The Frozen Fountain* (1932). The illustrations of these books were more of interest as a record of art deco imagery and architectural motifs than for their inventiveness. The visionary abstracted skyscraper renderings by Hugh Ferriss in *The Metropolis of Tomorrow*, which bore affinities to modernist theatrical stage settings and symbolic lighting, made even the most unlikely architectural ideas seem somehow possible.

The modernist stylization of art deco also extended to the witty caricatures of Mexican-born Miguel Covarrubias. After his 1923 arrival in New York, Covarrubias began to produce for *Vanity Fair*, *Vogue* and *The New Yorker* a series of abstracted watercolor and gouache (opaque watercolor) caricatures of the famous and infamous personalities of the times. In addition to designing sets and costumes for the theater, he also illustrated such books as W C Handy's *Treasury of the Blues* (1926); his own 1927 studies of Negro types, *Negro Drawings* (he was active in the social milieu of the Harlem Renaissance); and W H Hudson's *Green Mansions*. In the late 1930s, Covarrubias began a second career as a distinguished scholar and teacher of ethnology, anthropology and archaeology, primarily of the Indians of Mexico and Central America. The national archaeological museum in Mexico City was later named for him.

Another emigré who produced a notable body of art deco illustration was Greek-born John Vassos. After arriving in Boston in 1919, he studied art with John Singer Sargent and assisted stage designer Joseph Urban at the Boston Opera Company. His later commercial career in New York included window display design for leading department stores, murals for the Rialto and Rivoli theaters, advertising design for Packard and RCA, and the industrial design of such items as telephones, juke boxes, radio cabinets and soft drink dispensers.

Vassos is now recognized as one of America's most important practitioners of art deco style in advertising art and book illustration. In addition to illustrating such literary classics as Oscar Wilde's *Salomé*, *The Ballad of Reading Gaol* and *The Harlot's House*; Thomas Gray's *Elegy in a Country Church-Yard*; and Samuel Coleridge's *Kubla Khan*, Vassos produced, usually in collaboration with his wife Ruth Vassos who supplied the texts, several remarkable original works. These included the 1929 *Contempo*, an indictment of contemporary American culture and rampant commercialism; the 1930 *Ultimo: An Imaginative Narration of Life Under the Earth*; the 1931 *Phobia*, a study of psychic disorders; and the 1935 *Humanities*, an indictment of war. Vassos' dramatic illustrations for these books, executed in black, gray and white gouache, incorporated many stylistic devices of art deco – the decorative abstraction of human forms, nature and architecture; the rhythmic repetition of curves, diagonals and geometric shapes; and the frequent use of oblique or unusual viewpoints. Vassos' silhouette or montage-like compositions apparently were an eagerly awaited source of inspiration for Hollywood designers. His satirical psychological and sociological subject matter also points out that not all art deco design could be classified as merely superficial ornament, but that it could be effectively employed to explore the intellectual and political ideas of the age.

A wider audience was reached by those art deco artists doing illustrations for magazines and advertising clients. It is from these sources that the archetypal figures of the 1920s – the flapper and the Arrow Collar man – originated. That ideal sophisticated male of the jazz age, the Arrow Collar man, was created by German-born J C Leyendecker, who had studied for two years at the Academie Julian in Paris before his 1900 return to United States where he rapidly became New York's most prominent commercial illustrator. In his 1920s illustrations Leyendecker, whose Arrow Collar man reportedly was sent more love letters than Rudolf Valentino, employed dramatic contrasts of light and dark, combined with decorative color and figural stylization in a conservative style that reflected, nevertheless, art deco practices.

The frivolous and frenetic quality of the 1920s was explored, in a frequently satirical way, by the black and white drawings and the colorful magazine covers and posters of John Held, Jr. Held, who also worked as a painter, sculptor, theatrical costume and set designer, and a writer, demonstrated in his illustrations and posters an understanding of cubist ideas, and at times incorporated the zigzags, diagonals, figural stylization, abstract shapes and vivid colors of modernism in his cartoon-like renderings of Flaming Youth.

Art deco imagery dominated the covers of most magazines with any pretense of being modern. Credited with creating the 'flapper' – the quintessential 1920s woman – Neysa McMein designed all of the *McCall's* magazine covers between 1923 and 1937. Another prominent illustrator was Fish (Mrs Walter Sefton) who designed covers for *Vanity Fair*. Probably the record for the greatest number of magazine covers for a single publication was held by Ilonka Karasz, who executed 186 covers for *The New Yorker* between 1925 and 1973. Active in all areas of modern design – including furniture, silverware, textiles, wallpaper and ceramics – Karasz designed *New Yorker* covers during the 1920s that combined the typical imagery, stylization, repetitive patterns, vibrant colors and dynamic diagonals of the art deco style.

The most flamboyant of the magazine illustrators was the self-taught Gordon Conway who left rural Texas for Europe, where she became the toast of London during the last social season before World War I. In her studios in London and Paris, Conway executed commissions for Parisian plays, British films, and American manufacturers and magazines. Her sophisticated stylized jazz-era woman, particularly as seen in her *Zina* and *Jazz Lint* series, epitomized the spirit of the age. That the jazz age illustration style was ubiquitous during the 1920s could be seen in the early work done by that staunch propagandist and practitioner of the 1930s streamlined style, Raymond Loewy. Loewy's advertising assignments for such prestigious clients as Bonwit Teller and Neiman Marcus department stores were replete with lithe flappers, bounding greyhounds and rearing gazelles.

Harper's Bazaar magazine signed the leading spirit of Parisian art deco, Erté (the Russian-born, French-educated Romain de Tirtoff) to an exclusive contract from 1924 to 1937 to design magazine covers and fashion illustrations. Erté, who had also executed theater sets and dress designs, created stylized modernist covers with an elegant European flair. With designers such as Parisian Paul Poiret and Erté rendering their own fashion designs, fashion illustration had become a specialized and widely appreciated art form. The exotic orientalist decorativeness of many of Erté's fashion design illustrations probably evolved from the exotic ballet costume designs and sets created by Leon Bakst for the Ballets Russes. The 1909 Paris premiere of Diaghilev's dance company had had far-reaching results in transforming the colors, shapes and styles of the French fashion and design world.

The orientalism introduced by Leon Bakst's designs had already surfaced in the United States before Erté's

Below: Winold Reiss, invitation for Opportunity Award Dinner, 1925.

arrival. The tragically short-lived George R M Heppenstall worked on a series of splendidly patterned elegant drawings, incorporating oriental motifs in preparation for several projected books, among them *The Arabian Nights* and Oscar Wilde's *The House Of Pomegranates*. As a child, Heppenstall had been stimulated by Edmond Dulac's illustrations for *The Arabian Nights* and Omar Khayyam's *Rubaiyat*. He later worked with Nicholas Roerich, who had collaborated with Igor Stravinsky on the 1913 Diaghilev ballet production of *Le Sacre de Printemps*. During his three year professional career, Heppenstall produced designs for Broadway plays, oriental costumes for the Ziegfeld Follies, and dress designs for Lady Duff Gordon's fashion house.

In general, American illustration and graphic design remained relatively conservative, although there were some notable exceptions. A greater interest in modernist concepts in graphic design was demonstrated by two other early immigrant artists. Alfonso Iannelli, who arrived from Italy in 1898, studied sculpture under Gutzon Borglum at New York's Art Students League, and produced designs for *Harper's Weekly* and *Ladies Home Journal*. In 1910 he traveled to Los Angeles, where he designed over 100 vaudeville posters for the Orpheum Theater. These eye-catching cubist-influenced illustrations which were in the vanguard of American design of the era, brought him to the notice of Frank Lloyd Wright. Iannelli came to play a major role as a sculptor for Wright's Midway Gardens project, and he later collaborated with others – Bruce Goff, Barry Byrne and other Prairie School architects – designing for them not only sculpture but also light fixtures and other interior accessories.

Winold Reiss, who came to the United States from Germany in 1913, was also interested in pursuing modernist ideas. Active throughout his professional life not only as a graphic designer, but also as an interior and mural designer, Reiss immediately founded in New York City his own art school which remained active until 1933. In 1915 he helped publish twelve issues of the magazine, *Modern Art Collector*, whose color reproductions revolutionized the American printing industry. Reiss was particularly drawn to the decorative aspects of ethnographic, folk and American Indian art, and he incorporated motifs from these various sources into his own art deco designs. Reiss also became an active participant in the Harlem Renaissance. He provided illustrations for *The New Negro* (1925), a sumptuous poetry and prose anthology, and for other important publications of the black arts resurgence. And he also served as a teacher to Aaron Douglas and other black artists, ironically introducing Afro-Americans to African art.

In fact, Aaron Douglas, who became a leading painter of the Harlem Renaissance and in the following decade an important muralist executing New Deal projects, was also a significant art deco illustrator. He contributed six illus-

trations to *The New Negro*, and illustrated James Weldon Johnson's *God's Trombones: Seven Negro Sermons in Verse* (1927). His highly stylized drawings also appeared in such publications as *Vanity Fair*, *Theatre Arts Monthly*, *Opportunity*, and in Harlem's 'little magazines' *Harlem* and *Fire*.

As patrons who commissioned poster designs, theaters were generally more conservative than fashionable magazines, advertising clients and department stores. During the early decades of the twentieth century, the rapid rise of the motion picture had placed the live theater under some stress, as both were competing for the same audiences. In an attempt to provide an alternative to the level of drama that could be viewed on the neighborhood film screen, the experimental Theatre Guild was founded in New York City. The aim of this organization was to present to the United States public the latest works of leading avant-garde European and American playwrights. Thus, works that might not have ordinarily made their way to Broadway, by Luigi Pirandello, Ferenc Molnar, George Bernard Shaw and other innovative dramatists, were given a forum. The Theatre Guild also first produced the work of such upcoming American dramatists as Eugene O'Neill and Robert Sherwood.

Accordingly in its advertising, the Theatre Guild preferred modernist designs and commissioned work by

Left: Ilonka Karasz, cover illustration for *New Yorker* magazine, 10 October 1925.
Right: *George R M Heppenstall, Medea, 1922.*

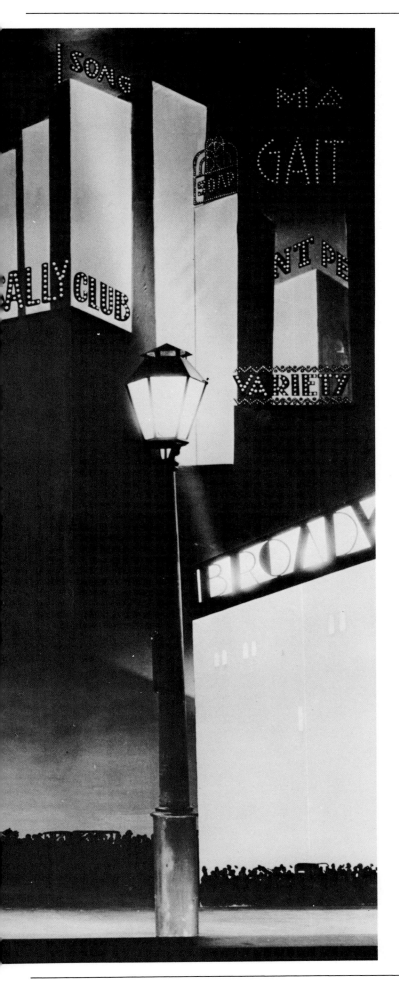

avant-garde European and American artists. The Guild posters initiated in the New York theater world modernist-influenced silkscreened prints of vivid and decorative areas of flat color, incorporating dynamic diagonals of shape, line and often bold hand lettering by the artist.

The striking and simplified designs of such early Theatre Guild designers as Fornaro – *Tea for Three* (1918), *The Bad Man* (1920), *Bluebeard's Eighth Wife* (1921), *Don Juan* (1921) and A A Milne's *Mr Pim Passes By* (1921) – reportedly often attracted audiences solely on the basis of the poster design. In the 1930s Frank Walts carried on the Fornaro tradition, notably in his designs for such productions as *Reunion in Vienna* (1931) and *The Taming of the Shrew* (1935). The Theatre Guild also commissioned designs by deserving unknowns such as art student Alexander Calder, whose 1925 lively silkscreened poster for Molnar's *The Glass Slipper* incorporated a stylization and decorative use of color similar to that used by such French artists as Henri Matisse. At this time, Calder had not yet made his first trip to Paris.

Another important poster designer was the Theatre Guild's leading set designer, Lee Simonson. Simonson, who originally studied drama at Harvard University, later went to Paris to study painting. As a member of the avant-garde circle of Gertrude Stein there, Simonson was introduced to modernism by the paintings of Cezanne, Picasso and Matisse, and by the theatrical experiments of the Ballets Russes and of Max Reinhardt. During his career as a successful stage designer in the 1920s, Simonson also made significant contributions to the art of theater poster design with his bold use of vibrant colors, decorative motifs, dynamic diagonals and hand lettering.

In the 1930s the design possibilities for theater posters began to be limited by the rise of the star system and the required inclusion of numerous production credits. In the previous decade, actors' names had not been considered essential information on Theatre Guild play advertising. But the later need to add the names of all these contributing to the production caused the printed text to dominate the visual design. Some designers, such as Frank Walts and John Held, Jr, (in his poster designs for *Boy Meets Girl and What a Life*) were able cleverly to combine both word and image into an effective unified design, but in many cases the visual material was limited to caricatures of the players, or even to ornamental borders.

But some of the modernist motifs and aesthetic emphasis seen in early Theatre Guild posters were revived in the products of the New Deal Works Progress Administration (WPA) Poster Project. This federally-sponsored commercial art program, which lasted from 1935 to 1942, produced posters for various governmental agencies, among them another WPA program – The Federal Theater Project. By this time the American art world had become reinfused with European modernist ideas with the immigration of numerous top graphic designers fleeing the political uncertainties of Europe.

Above: Federal Theatre Project for *Help Yourself*, WPA Poster Project.

Hence, many of the WPA posters for the Federal Theater Project (which, like the Theatre Guild, was not required to list extensive production credits) could emphasize visual imagery and unified design based on constructivist and other modernist graphic design principles. A goodly number of the Federal Theater Project posters, many of them by unknown designers, were in the forefront of avant-garde design – often including the severely simplified figures; the rhythmic repetition of curves, lines and geometric shapes; and the bold dynamic diagonals that featured so prominently in art deco design.

Much less experimentation and abstraction was permitted in those posters and other graphic designs used by the motion picture industry for advertising purposes. In

Europe, film was regarded more as a legitimate art form and its graphic imagery reflected that perception. In the United States, film was treated more as a commercial product to be sold to the masses. Thus, in American posters the emphasis was on promoting the star. The artists were not permitted to design works in an individualistic fashion; and in most cases they were even denied credit for those designs they did produce. The result was a relatively conservative homogeneity. At the end of the 1920s, a little more latitude for experimentation was permitted and a number of the posters of those and succeeding years had a more boldly dynamic quality, resulting from the use of such modernist techniques as varied lettering sizes, styles and placement; the frequent use of dramatic diagonals of line and contour; the patterned repetition of motifs; and the use of vivid and broad areas of color.

The iconography of art deco was frequently seen in these posters – such as airplanes in *Wings* (1927), *Hells Angels* (1930), *Flying Down to Rio* and *King Kong* (1933). The *King Kong* poster also included a dramatically oblique bird's eye view of New York skyscrapers, the

Below: *The Emperor's New Clothes*, WPA Poster Project. Art deco's flat colors and simplified contours changed traditional imagery.

Top left: Joseph Binder, *Air Corps US Army*, 1941.
Left: *$1,300 for One Bomb*, World Peace Posters, 1931.
Above: Alexander Calder, *The Glass Slipper*, 1925.

Chrysler building among them. John Held, Jr was one of the few artists to break the barrier of movie poster design anonymity. MGM's *Tin Hats* (1926) and *Good Times* (1930) posters displayed Held's characteristic flappers. (Thomas Hart Benton, for the 1939 *Grapes of Wrath*, and Norman Rockwell, for the 1942 *The Magnificent Ambersons*, were also among the artists allowed to design in their own individual styles.) During the World War II years, the Hollywood studios experienced their greatest prosperity to date, but in the postwar decades experiment in poster design – conservative though it may have been – declined as color photographs, combined with stock lettering, came to dominate the movie poster.

Above: Jean Carlu, *Give 'Em Both Barrels*, 1941.

Meanwhile, the influx of foreign graphic artists began to transform other aspects of the communications arts. As had long been the case, fashion magazines were in the forefront of design developments. Condé Nast updated the look of his publications, including *Vogue, Vanity Fair* and *House and Garden*, by hiring as art director in the late 1920s Dr Mehemed Fehmy Agha, a Ukrainian-born Turk who had studied in Kiev and worked as a graphic artist in Paris and Berlin. William Randolph Hearst's *Harper's Bazaar* was revitalized in the early 1930s by the appointment of Russian emigre Alexey Brodovich as art director. The inventive Brodovich, originally a French graphic designer and a set designer for the Ballets Russes, instituted revolutionary changes in the graphic design of the magazine by utilizing large areas of empty space to dynamically and rhythmically balance the blocks of text, photographs and artwork. He also drew on montage and other modernist techniques to juxtapose, enlarge or crop images for dramatic effect. Brodovich frequently commissioned other important and influential avant-garde designers, artists and photographers such as Man Ray, Salvador Dali and Henri Cartier Bresson to produce works for *Harper's.*

He also hired the noted Parisian art deco graphic

designer A M Cassandre to design a series of covers. In the 1920s and 1930s, Cassandre – through his bold stylized images emphasizing two-dimensionality, broad planes of color, and adept integration of image with word in innovative typefaces often designed by himself – had almost singlehandedly raised French graphic design to an internationally admired art form. Among his most notable posters were those done for the French railroad and steamship companies. While in the United States, Cassandre also executed commissions for other clients, among them the Container Corporation of America and W W Ayer. He returned to Paris in 1939.

The Container Corporation of America played a unique role in the American modern design movement during the 1930s. The company head, Chicagoan Walter P Paepcke, held the enlightened view that with innovative design a business could increase profits and at the same time support cultural advances. In 1936 he hired as design director Egbert Jacobsen to oversee the complete overhaul of the company's visual design – its industrial interiors, trademark logo, stationery and printed materials, and advertising. Cassandre's advertising designs for the firm revolutionized traditional American industrial advertising, which hitherto had relied on long wordy texts. Cassandre designed instead a dramatic and simple central image accompanied by a very minimal text.

When Cassandre returned to France the Container Corporation went on to commission advertisements by other important artists and designers, among them Herbert Bayer, Jean Carlu, Fernand Leger, Herbert Matter and Man Ray. Paepcke, who admired the Bauhaus, also provided essential financial support for Laszlo Moholy-Nagy's Institute of Design in Chicago.

Yet another important graphic designer who came to America in the late 1930s was E McKnight Kauffer, who was originally an American born in Montana. Kauffer, who had left the country to study art in Europe after seeing the Armory Show when it traveled to Chicago, achieved an important reputation in London with his cubist-influenced posters (141 of them for London Underground Transport) and other graphic designs. During World War II, the United States government Office of War Information commissioned Kauffer to design a series of posters to raise the morale of those European countries occupied by the enemy.

The designers of the WPA Poster Project (mentioned earlier in connection with theater posters) were strongly influenced by recent European design developments, particularly the Russian constructivist incorporation of type as an abstract design element and the bold simplified images of Cassandre and others. These kinds of designs were especially suited to the silkscreen technique used for most WPA work. The Poster Project supervisor, Richard Floethe, himself had studied design at the Bauhaus, and he impressed the project designers with the utilitarian intent of these posters which were created for a wide variety of federal state and civic agencies to promote education, housing, health issues, crime prevention and government-sponsored cultural events.

The design principles absorbed by the Poster Project artists were employed by other commercial artists as well to produce striking graphic images for such items as record album covers, printed music covers, book jackets and even billboards. Notable among the independent American designers in the late 1930s was Lester Beall, a self-taught graphic artist, who worked first in Chicago and then in New York. In his posters for such clients as the Rural Electrification Administration, Beall effectively combined simple dramatic visuals with flat geometric areas of color, for a two-dimensional effect. He also experimented with collage-like effects by incorporating photographic imagery and even nineteenth-century wood typefaces into his designs. The inventive Beall valued the role of intuition in graphic design as equal to that of rational order.

As war broke out in Europe, many leading graphic designers lent their talents to the creation of propaganda for the Allies. Antiwar posters, most of them by anonymous artists, had been produced since the 1920s. These too gained impact from the use of bold, simplified art deco designs.

Viennese designer Joseph Binder, who had been in New York since 1935, began to use the airbrush to modulate his flat shapes in a smooth, mechanistic way. Bauhaus designer, Herbert Bayer, who came to New York in 1938, also experimented with the airbrush to enhance his stylized mask-like rendering of faces and in conjunction

Above: Lester Beall, *Radio, Rural Electrification Administration,* 1937, silkscreen.

with his montage-like designs. The airbrush, which was originally used by photographers as a retouching tool, was also used by commercial art illustrators to produce flawless surfaces and to effect a realistic sense of volume. This technique was particularly effective in the hands of Binder, Jean Carlu and other modernist graphic designers who used the airbrush to achieve perfect qualities of finish on geometrized art deco shapes.

Binder created one of his finest designs, promoting the United States Army Air Corps, for the United States Office of War Information. And noted French graphic artist, Jean Carlu, who was stranded in America by the German capture of Paris, also produced some of his finest designs for the Allied war effort. One of his posters promoting industrial productivity in support of the nation's massive military build-up won first prize in a government-sponsored competition and brought Carlu other professional honors in the United States as well. This application of art deco graphic design to a variety of uses, from commercial advertising to war propaganda, underlines not only the style's symbolic power, but also its adaptability to media besides architectural, interior and furniture design.

5
CERAMICS, GLASS, METALWARE, PLASTICS

By the time of the art deco era, art pottery makers had become securely entrenched in the United States as a result of the growth of the Arts and Crafts movement, which had begun around the time of the 1876 Philadelphia Centennial Exposition and extended through the first world war. The American Arts and Crafts movement had its roots in England, where John Ruskin and William Morris proposed a renewal of the decorative arts with an emphasis on fine handwork by trained craftsmen, similar to those of the middle ages. This movement was in large part a reaction against industrialism, the impersonal manufactures of the machine, and the loss of the worker's control over the end products of his labor. American enthusiasm for these ideas led to the establishment of such ceramics works as Cincinnati's Rookwood Pottery in 1880; Chelsea Pottery in Chelsea, Massachusetts, in 1891; Newcomb Pottery in New Orleans in 1895; Dedham Pottery in Dedham, Massachusetts, in 1896; Pewabic Pottery in Detroit in 1903; and Indiana's Overbeck Pottery in 1911.

It is notable that the American art pottery movement offered a unique opportunity for women to participate as productive artists to an extent hitherto impossible. And women were involved on the business side as well – the phenomenally successful Rookwood Pottery was founded by Maria Longworth Nichols, Pewabic Pottery by May Chase Perry, and Overbeck Pottery by the four Overbeck sisters. Widespread participation by women in this medium also extended through the art deco decades of the 1920s and 1930s.

Also of significance was the fact that many of the pottery works were located outside the metropolitan centers of modern design. Many of them were organized in Ohio, the midwest and the south, establishing the heartland of America as a source of high quality design. Medals awarded to American ceramists at numerous international expositions also encouraged this perception.

And unlike many modern painters and sculptors, ceramists continued to flourish during the late 1920s and

1930s. They produced a relatively inexpensive, original, and widely appreciated art form that did not have to rely on the patronage of art museums and galleries. Ceramics had followed a course apart from the mainstream of modern art, with its own specialized exhibition opportunities, resulting in an independent structure of patron-

Below: At Steuben Glass, Carder's art nouveau line ceded to art deco.

Left: Noritake art deco porcelain, *Masquerade*, wall pocket.

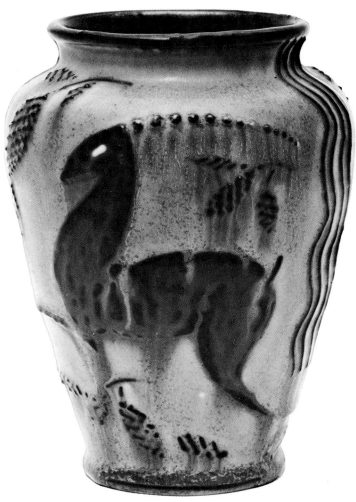

Above: Jens Jensen, Rookwood vase, 1934.

age. The native American-born potters, many of whom saw themselves as preserving craft traditions in the face of modern machine production, were supplemented in the 1920s and 1930s by immigrant European-born or trained ceramists, many of whom regarded themselves as allied in intent to contemporary painters and sculptors. The artist-craftspeople holding this attitude were more apt to adapt art deco motifs in their work.

During the late nineteenth century, experiments in technique, color, and glaze gave visualization to a variety of historically-based and orientally-influenced designs. As the nation entered the modern era after World War I, the sinuous floral and flowing organic motifs of the predominant art nouveau style gave way, in a select group of works, to the conventionalized floral patterns, geometric cubist designs and other art deco imagery, as consciously modern ceramists followed the lead of French art deco potters. And in 1928 the International Exhibition of Ceramic Art at New York's Metropolitan Museum of Art found American ceramists as technically accomplished as the Europeans.

Rookwood Pottery, whose success had attracted a number of imitators in nearby Zanesville, Ohio (which became known as "Clay City"), remained relatively immune to the new art deco style and continued to produce its highly regarded line of naturalistic plants and

animals on pots with smooth underglazes applied in subtle transitions of color. A one-of-a-kind vase by Jens Jensen with a brown gazelle in raised slip on a turquoise ground was probably the closest Rookwood came to art deco. The fine execution of this elegant piece was characteristic of Rookwood's high standards of production and artistic quality. An immigrant to the United States, Danish artist Jensen worked for Rookwood from 1928 to 1948 and produced designs in a variety of styles for the company. Though not as self consciously modernistic as that made by other ceramics concerns, Rookwood pottery continued in wide demand throughout the decades between the wars. Indeed, America's greatest hero of the era, aviator Charles Lindbergh, was presented with a valuable Rookwood vase.

Rookwood's major followers in Zanesville, Ohio, were Weller Pottery and Rosewood Pottery. Around 1920, Weller's catalogs included a variety of items – including vases, bowls, and candlesticks – in the art deco Paragon pattern of incised, stylized leaves and flowers. The early date of the Paragon bowl (around 1919) shows that such art deco designs were available in the United States well before the 1925 Paris exposition. The explanation for this may lie in the fact that Weller's art director from 1905 to 1920 was Englishman Frederick Alfred Rhead, who had previously worked in various British potteries, among them the exclusive Minton factory. Weller's Paragon pattern also resembled art glass being produced in France and Germany at the time. Weller's Manhattan pattern, and various novelty items such as a vertically striped coffee service and tumblers painted with stylized faces (both also of 1919) were other examples of the company's art deco items. Rosewood Pottery also produced stylized floral and foliage patterns such as Clemana, Baneda, and Morning Glory which in their asymmetrical composition were transitional between art nouveau and art deco. Rosewood Pottery also hired European talent such as Danish designer Christian Neilson, who had studied sculpture at Copenhagen's Royal Academy of Art.

Overbeck Pottery was established in Cambridge City, Indiana, in 1911 by the four Overbeck sisters, two of whom had studied with Columbia University's Arthur

Below: Overbeck Pottery, art deco tea set, earthenware.

Wesley Dow, an influential art educator who had also taught Georgia O'Keeffe and other modernists. Much of the output of Overbeck pottery combined art deco patterns and shapes. Their earthenware, hand-built tea sets were a prime example of this. The angular silhouettes of the vessels provided an appropriate setting for either incised or colored abstract cubist-inspired designs of circles, squares, and diamonds. Overbeck also produced stylized animal and figure patterns, an important example of which was a 1934 bowl and stand with a continuous encircling scene of incised conventionalized of dancing couples. This bowl was made under the auspices of the New Deal Public Works Administration.

Obviously, American craftspeople and the American public were familiar with the art deco style originating from France in the years preceding the 1925 Paris exposition. But the very important 1928 international ceramic art exhibit at the Metropolitan Museum of Art introduced to many Americans the sophisticated clay work by Austrian artists from the Wiener Werkstätte. The witty Viennese figural ceramics were regarded by many as the finest examples of modern design to come out of Europe, though there were some American critics who disapproved of their 'frivolity,' a quality that was nevertheless so characteristic of the roaring twenties. Following the 1928 Metropolitan exhibition, a number of American ceramists traveled to Vienna to study their craft.

The most famous of these Americans was Viktor Schreckengost from Sebring, Ohio. After an education at the Cleveland Institute of Arts, he studied ceramics and sculpture at the Kunstgewerbeschule under Michael Powolny from 1929 to 1930. While in Vienna, Schreckengost developed an interest in the Viennese specialty of large scale clay figural sculpture. This interest was also to spread to American ceramics circles with the arrival in the United States of the important Viennese ceramist Vally Wieselthier, of whom more later.

Schreckengost was persuaded to return to the United States by pottery manufacturer R Guy Cowan, who recruited him for a job at his Cowan Pottery Studio located in the Cleveland suburb of Rocky River. This new position also permitted Schreckengost to teach part time at the Cleveland School of Art. Despite Cowan Pottery's need to mass produce such items as vases, candlesticks, and centerpieces, Schreckengost was also allowed freedom to experiment, and an impressive result was his 1931 set of 20 punch bowls decorated with images representing New Year's Eve in New York City. Produced in two sizes and available in a variety of colors, a number of these punch bowls were purchased by Eleanor Roosevelt for entertaining in the New York governor's mansion. Decorated in a graffito (scratched-on) technique, each bowl had a different design based on a dynamic interpretation of contemporary social life. The stylized, cubist-inspired images

Below: Vally Wieselthier, ceramic sculpture.

Below: Vally Wieselthier, *Taming the Unicorn*, ceramic sculpture.

Left: Waylande Gregory, *Margarita*, 1929, glazed porcelain.
Above left and right: The nature imagery on the Arts and Crafts Moravian tile and Weller pitcher was adapted later by art deco designers.

of skyscrapers, cocktail glasses, bottles and other motifs from the 1920s were interspersed with such evocative words as 'follies,' 'dance,' and 'jazz,' in syncopated lettering. Schreckengost reported that his primary influence for this frothy mixture of words and images was the Vienna poster work of designer Joseph Binder. A mass produced version of the punch bowls, with carved decoration, was later made available.

Below left: Weller Pottery, Paragon pattern bowl.
Below right: Viktor Schreckengost, punch bowl, 1931.

A similar combination of Viennese liveliness and American-scene imagery was also seen in Schreckengost's set of six plates with sporting themes in molded relief. The exuberant, stylized figures portrayed playing football, polo, golf, and tennis, and hunting and swimming, were close in spirit to those drawn by John Held, Jr. During the 1930s Schreckengost continued to work in this whimsical vein in conscious reaction, according to him, against the general gloom of the depression.

As noted earlier, Vally Wieselthier, the head of the ceramics workshop of the Wiener Werkstätte and one of the most important European ceramists of the twenties, moved to the United States in 1929. She joined the New York City decorative arts group, Contempora, for which she designed glass, textiles, papier-mâché department

Above: Maija Grotell, vase, 1940, glazed earthenware.
Above right: Maija Grotell, *The City*, circa 1930.

store mannequins, and the metal elevator doors for Ely Jacques Kahn's Squibb Building. She also designed ceramics for Sebring Pottery in Ohio and also continued to produce from her New York studio her large scale ceramic sculptures of flappers and other stylized figures. These works had an important influence on the development of ceramic sculpture in the United States during the 1930s. And, as did Schreckengost, Wieselthier saw her decorative sculpture, so expressive of the joy of life, as an antidote to the dreariness of the depression.

Wieselthier's effective promotion of ceramic sculpture as a valid art form led such important artists as Alexander Archipenko, Elie Nadelman, and Isamu Noguchi also to try their hand at clay sculpture. A considerable attraction of clay as a medium was its relatively low cost in comparison to other materials such as stone and metal during economic hard times. An artist who left the medium of bronze to become a major ceramist of the era was Waylande Gregory. Gregory had studied with sculptor Lorado Taft at the Art Institute of Chicago and in Florence, Italy. After he joined Cowan Pottery, he designed a number of sylph-like ceramic figures of women, among which was his 1929 *Margarita*. These figures, with their simple stylized elegance of line and their graceful elongated proportions, were part of an important sub genre of art deco. Some of Cowan Pottery's later statuettes of this nature were apparently indebted to the ideas of sculptor Paul Manship,

who rendered several such designs for the company in the last years of its operation.

As Cowan Pottery began to falter in the early 1930s, Gregory went on to become artist in residence at Cranbrook Academy from 1932 to 1933. During that time, he developed Cranbrook's first organized ceramics program, but discord with Cranbrook administration and other faculty members led to Gregory's precipitate departure. The ceramic sculptures he had created during his short stay at Cranbrook gained national recognition for Gregory, as he continued to exhibit them in various exhibitions throughout the 1930s. Gregory later established his own studio in Bound Brook, New Jersey. His most monumental ceramic sculpture was *The Fountain of Atoms* (1938), in which each of the twelve ceramic figures – *Fire, Earth, Air, Water* and the eight *Electrons* – each weighed over a ton. The impressive size of these pieces was made possible by Gregory's unusual hand-building method, a remarkable technical innovation, in which he built up the sculptures in an interior honeycomb pattern. The cosmic imagery and the monumentalism of the sculpture fit into the art deco canon – recalling the astrological imagery often seen in skyscraper lobbies, and reflecting the conscious monumentalism of New Deal sculpture and architecture. *The Fountain of Atoms*, was exhibited, as were many other art deco sculptures and murals, at the 1939 New York World's Fair.

The departure of Gregory left Cranbrook Academy with no official ceramics program until 1938, when Finnish-born artist-potter Maija Grotell took over the

Above: Sargent Johnson, *Negro Woman*, 1933, terra cotta.

direction of the department. Grotell, who had studied painting, sculpture, and design at Helsinki's School of Industrial Art, spent the following six years working under the important European potter Alfred William Finch. She immigrated to the United States in 1927. After teaching at New York's Henry Street Settlement House, she became a pottery instructor at New Jersey's Rutgers University School of Ceramic Engineering.

Grotell's earlier artistic output in the United States included simple cylindrical vases with painted-on art deco designs in a decorative cubist style. Her 1935 earthenware vase, *The City*, was an example of such work. Here the motifs were the same as those explored by precisionist painters and photographers of the era – skyscraper skylines, steamships and other transportation vehicles, and the geometric aesthetic of machine and industrial forms. On other ceramic vessels, Grotell created more abstracted versions of the skyline and industrial motifs. She used a vivid range of colors, reflecting the interests of the synchromist painters and the decorative Parisian designs of Sonia Delaunay. Besides the urban scenes, Grotell also painted other lively images, including animal motifs, often in a simplified linear style.

Grotell's tenure at Cranbrook, where she was according to all accounts a stimulating and inspiring teacher, allowed her to develop her ideas more fully. The unusually large size of the Cranbrook kiln permitted her to produce more monumental and volumetric pots. A 1939

vase of simple horizontal bands on the spherical body of the vessel, accompanied by a checkerboard pattern on its cylindrical neck, combined cubist geometric volumes with the streamlined style motif of horizontal speed stripes.

This kind of evolutionary development was not apparent in Dorothy Warren O'Hara's 1939 earthenware bowl incised with an art deco bird pattern. Despite its relatively late date, this vessel, with its 1920s-style sharp-edged stylized motifs, made no accommodation to the intervening streamlined aesthetic. Evidently the cubist-influenced animal style of the twenties continued in demand well into the next decade. O'Hara had also studied abroad, in Munich, Paris, and London; and with J Pierpont Morgan as a patron, she found a ready market for her work on her return to the United States. Here she established a studio – first in New York City, and then in Darien, Connecticut – named Apple Tree Lane Pottery. Her distinctive vessels with their high relief modeling were purchased for the collections of major American museums. Earlier in her career, O'Hara also produced articles and illustrations for *Ladies Home Journal*.

The terra cotta heads of Negro women and children, also of the 1930s, by black San Francisco artist Sargent Johnson were representative of another subgenre of art deco design – stylized, mask-like sculptures of heads. Initially explored by modernist sculptors such as Elie Nadelman, Constantin Brancusi and Isamu Noguchi, this motif was also adapted by a number of important ceramists, including Viktor Schreckengost, A Drexler Jacobsen of Cowan Pottery, and others. With these heads, which he also made in copper, Sargent Johnson drew on African primitive art as an appropriate antecedent to express the growing pride of Afro-Americans in their ethnic origins. Such primitivist models also became an important source of inspiration for other painters and sculptors of the Harlem Renaissance, among them Aaron Douglas, Charles Alston, Archibald Motley, Richmond Barthé, and Augusta Savage. Johnson's heads were elegantly idealized; they depicted not individuals, but noble types representative of the dignity and rich heritage of the black race. Their resemblance to the portraits of ancient Egyptian pharaohs was more than coincidental. Their air of stately impassivity, coupled with the decorative treatment of the hair and stylized features emphasized the parallel. The recent opening in Egypt of Tutankhamen's tomb had helped to make Egyptian decorative ideas a popular art deco motif.

Born in Boston, Sargent Johnson had studied under Beniamino Bufano and Ralph Stackpole in San Francisco. His work in ceramics, metal sculpture, and mural bas-reliefs, which was inspired by synthetic cubism and Mexican art, as well as by that of Africa, attempted to show the 'natural beauty and dignity of the pure American Negro.' During the New Deal era of the 1930s, Johnson was appointed a senior sculpture supervisor for the Federal Arts Project in San Francisco.

Another kind of primitivism drawn on by art deco designers was that of American Indian art. Particularly influential were its abstracted geometric patterns, as seen in Navaho blankets, the jewelry and basketry of various tribes, and the pottery of the southwest. These items were,

Above: Dorothea Warren O'Hara, carved terra cotta bowl with black glaze, circa 1941.

of course, available to knowledgeable collectors, and became accessible to a wider audience with the publication of Franz Boas' profusely illustrated *Primitive Art.* Interest in American Indians and their art was further stimulated by the vast photographic documentation – a total of over 2200 images – of more than 80 western tribes from Alaska to Mexico completed by Edward S Curtis and published in 20 volumes between 1903 and 1930. In addition to the regal Indian portraits, Curtis also recorded their characteristic dress, ornamental beadwork, teepees painted with symbolic geometric designs, elegant basketry and other visually striking crafts in *The North American Indian.*

During the 1920s and 1930s, there was widespread appreciation for the work of the Indian potters of the American southwest, foremost among whom were Maria Martinez of San Idelfonso Pueblo, New Mexico; Tonita and Juan Roybal, also of San Idelfonso; Nampayo of the Hopi mesa in Hano, Arizona; and Lucy Lewis of Acoma, New Mexico. The indigenous geometric Hopi, Pueblo and Zuni designs which incorporated stylized bird, deer, flower, cloud, and lightning motifs frequently resembled and may have served as an inspiration for some art deco motifs. In any case, during the art deco era there arose a great demand for contemporary Indian ceramics based on the traditional patterns and techniques used by the potters of the southwest. Their pots, which had been created anonymously for centuries, now came to be individually signed by the more famous potters.

Probably the most highly respected of the potters was Maria Martinez who learned the craft of polychrome pot making from her aunt. When asked in 1908 to replicate a unique kind of black pottery from ancient shards found in a nearby archeological excavation site, Martinez rediscovered the traditional technique of making black-on-black ware by smothering the flames during firing with dried manure. But the Martinez pots – of a polished silvery black, with or without the matte black geometric patterns – were judged superior to those made by her ancestors. These wares, along with her polychrome pots, brought her worldwide fame. Her pottery – which was usually made in collaboration with her husband Julian, and after his death with her children and grandchildren – was shown at nearly every important exposition up to World War II, including the 1933 Chicago Century of Progress fair and the 1939 New York World of Tomorrow fair. Maria Martinez also personally demonstrated pottery-making at a number of these expositions. Her remarkable achievement brought her two honorary doctorates, White House invitations by four presidents, and the unusual tribute of being asked to lay the cornerstone for the construction of Rockefeller Center.

The earthenware plates and bowls made by Martinez in the 1920s and 1930s demonstrated the affinity of Pueblo Indian art and art deco patterns. The stylization of natural forms into geometrized shapes such as zigzags, triangles, and stepped-back patterns (resembling the skyscraper style) all paralleled the modernist abstraction practiced by art deco designers.

The American southwest also provided inspiration for European-trained designers working in the art deco style. A lively 1929 plate, *Cowboy Mounting Horse* by W Hunt Diederich recalled, in style if not subject matter, his other ceramic works which portrayed elegant, silhouetted greyhounds or ibex. Yet, in spirit, this subject matter deriving from the American west was humorously treated in a way similar to the somewhat frivolous, Viennese-influenced

Right: Noritake art deco porcelain, *Geometrics.*
Below: Noritake art deco porcelain, *Frond Fantasy Floral.*

Above: Maria Martinez, plate, circa 1939.

works of American art deco. Diederich had become interested in ceramics as an artistic medium while on a 1923 Moroccan trip. There the North African wares so impressed him that he immediately began painting his own designs on individual ceramic pieces, and he later began to design as well for mass production during the mid twenties. Diederich's *Cowboy* was perhaps a souvenir of a fondly remembered adolescent stint as a working cowboy in Arizona, New Mexico and Wyoming. Such regional adaptation of the art deco style was not unusual: Just as stylized cactus was a feature of Pueblo deco, so did palm trees, flamingos, and pelicans become part of the stylized

architectural decoration of the tropical deco of Old Miami Beach and Los Angeles, and of the Louisiana state capital building in Baton Rouge.

The international scope of art deco was emphasized by the production process of Noritake art deco porcelains, which were designed in New York City by a British art director for American buyers, were made in Japan, and then exported to the United States for sale. These Noritake porcelains were relatively low priced, of high quality and decorated with diverse imagery, making the latest art deco designs available to the broad American public. These porcelains were sold widely in department stores and gift shops across the nation from 1921 to 1941.

Their sophisticated and vivid imagery, designed in New

Above: W Hunt Diederich, *Cowboy Mounting Horse*, 1929.

York by a staff under the inspired leadership of Englishman Cyril Leigh, drew on the entire range of art deco motifs also seen in other media during those years – conventionalized floral and animal decoration, geometric cubist-influenced designs, stylized flappers and other elegant females similar to those seen in fashion illustrations, exotic vistas, decoration based on pre-Columbian artifacts, and vignettes of party life in the effervescent twenties. The wares – plates, vases, bowls, novelties and other forms – were produced by the mold process, and the shapes of the vessels were based on simple classical and neoclassical prototypes that provided an effective setting

for the vivid contrasting colors, glossy surfaces and bold hard-edged images that were later applied by hand.

The Japanese Noritake works, a subsidiary of Morimura Brothers, produced the so-called 'fancy ware' destined for export to western nations by utilizing the latest in mass production techniques. An assembly line of porcelain decorators painted the wares by hand, each completing a specific area of the total design. Although the designs were generally done almost wholly by hand in the 1920s, during the following decade the use of ceramic decals became more widespread, undoubtedly for economic reasons. With ceramic decals, the image fused to the surface of the vessel when it was fired in the kiln. Originally the decals had been employed to imprint the black

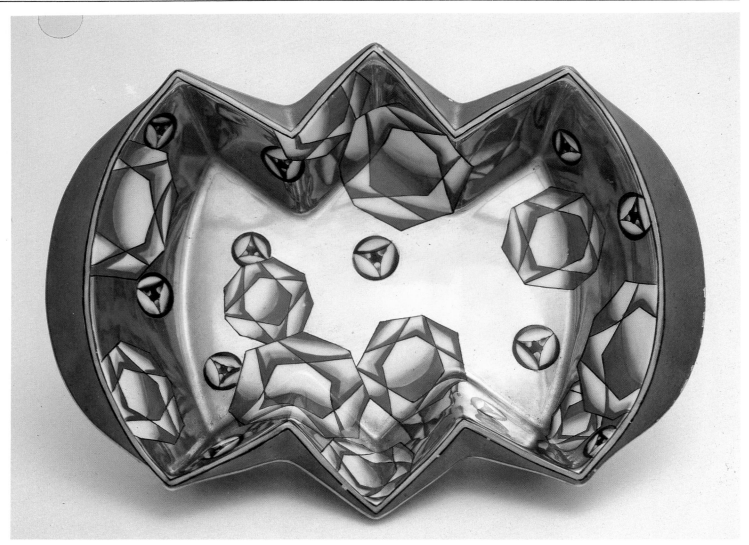

Above: Noritake art deco porcelain, *Jewels*.

outlines of the designs, which were subsequently painted in by hand, but in the final years of Noritake's art deco porcelain production, most of the decoration came to be applied by ceramic decal, with only a small amount of additional hand painting. Ceramic decals were, in effect, an ideal mass production technique.

Another characteristic of these porcelains was the frequent use of luster – an iridescent metallic surface treatment applied over the glaze to create either gold or silver opaque lusters, or transparent lusters of mother-of pearl and various other colors. Undoubtedly there was some connection between this use of metallic lusters, and the deep interest of art deco designers in the machine aesthetic. This is not to suggest, of course, that the use of iridescent finishes was unique to the art deco period. Similar sheens were used in the preceding art nouveau era, notably by Louis Tiffany in his acclaimed favrile glass.

The use of porcelain for the Noritake wares was in itself significant. Originally this hard and translucent ceramic substance (first discovered in China during the seventh or eighth century, and then rediscovered in 1709 by alchemist Johann Friedrich Böttger who later became director of the Meissen porcelain factory near Dresden)

had been reserved for those wares made exclusively for the aristocratic and wealthy. The democratizing social trends of the twentieth century thus were reflected in the removal of porcelain from such elite status.

As the 1920s gave way to the 1930s, changes in the nature and content of the applied designs also occurred. While the imagery of the 1920s was dynamic, diverse, exuberant, and executed in vivid arbitrary colors, the designs of the depression-era 1930s tended to be more restrained and more symmetrical. Also apparent was a greater use of all-over patterns. The conservatism of the Noritake porcelains of the 1930s paralleled developments in art deco design elsewhere. Hence, the large body of Noritake art deco porcelains produced during the 1920s and 1930s becomes a remarkable visual record of not only the fashion trends, life styles, and art movements of the era, but also of its social changes.

The standards of high quality consistently maintained by Noritake brought it yet another American client. Frank Lloyd Wright, who had insisted early in his career that the whole architectural environment must be considered an integral unit, commanded the total design of his Tokyo Imperial Hotel (1922) by also designing the

Right: The sauceboat, shakers and sugar bowl in the near column are Harlequin ware; the plates and tumbler are Fiesta ware.

china to be used by the hotel customers. In his previous commissions in the United States, Wright had designed such accoutrements to his buildings as stained glass windows, ironwork gates, furniture, lamps, vases and candlesticks — many of them in the then-current austere and linear Arts and Crafts style. The forward-looking-Wright had declared in a 1901 speech, long before it was acceptable to do so, that he saw the machine as a reasonable and desirable means of producing well-designed household furniture and related decorative arts objects. The mass production techniques employed by Noritake, therefore, had Wright's stamp of approval.

The Noritake-made Tokyo Imperial Hotel china indicated Wright's sensitivity to contemporary trends of style — the design of the dinnerware fit comfortably into the art deco canon of the 1920s. As was customary with Noritake ware, the forms of the dishes were classically simple, in contrast to their modernistic, cubist-like applied imagery. Wright's lively geometric design of colorful spheres and hemispheres bore a close affinity to Sonia Delaunay's Parisian *pochoir* and textile designs. The motif that was seen on the dinnerware was also included in the interior design of the Imperial Hotel — in a mural over the fireplace.

Wright lived in Japan from 1916 to 1922, and he was interested in Japanese art; in fact, he accumulated a fine collection of Japanese prints. But his china and mural design for the Tokyo Imperial Hotel seemed only peripherally related to Japanese artistic ideas — there is a suggestion of oriental aesthetic, perhaps, in the design's deliberate asymmetry and the large expanse left completely free of any imagery or color. It must be noted, however, that Wright had created a remarkably similar design some ten years earlier in his 1912 multicolored leaded glass windows for the Avery Coonley Playhouse in Riverside, Illinois. Indeed, these windows, with their asymmetrical nonobjective design of spherical and geometric shapes, and their sensitive balancing of shape, color and void, were a noteworthy forerunner of art deco.

Frank Lloyd Wright's first major industrial commission had come in 1903 from the Larkin Company of Buffalo, New York. Not only did he create a radical, almost futuristic design for the soap company building, but he also designed appropriate furniture and other accessories for the corporate offices. It is also possible that he may have designed such ceramic items as cuspidors for the Larkin building. At any rate, the cuspidors were manufactured by Buffalo Pottery, a subsidiary company founded by the Larkin Company in 1901 to mass produce dishes and other ceramic items, initially for use as premiums to increase sales of the company's soap products. This innovative marketing strategy was developed by Larkin's promotional genius, Elbert Hubbard. During the 1930s, the practice of giving away premiums became widespread as vendors of all kinds of products sought to stimulate sales in a depressed economy; many of the depression-era premiums were art deco ceramics and glassware. The charismatic Elbert Hubbard later became the leader of Roycroft, an important Arts and Crafts community near Buffalo.

In 1917, Buffalo Pottery began the production of high quality institutional dinner services for a wide variety of clients, including private clubs, hotels, restaurants, railroads and steamships. The majority of Buffalo's institutional wares predictably were based on historical revival styles. But a selected number of the designs, including some for railroads and other enlightened clients, incorporated geometric art deco, or streamlined motifs, such as speeding locomotives. Buffalo Pottery maintained an interest in modernistic ideas throughout the art deco era, as may be seen from the fact that the company commissioned Ilonka Karasz during the mid 1930s to create a number of ceramic designs, including one for a simplified teapot and samovar that employed the cubist geometric vocabulary of the sphere and cylinder.

The creation of well-designed household, and later institutional, dinnerware was also a goal pursued by Russel Wright, whose design career lasted over 30 years. During these decades, he devised, in addition to his furniture and textile lines, 11 lines of ceramic dinnerware and later on, two lines of plastic dinnerware. Wright stood apart from most of the industrial designers of the 1930s in that his energy was primarily directed toward the design of household furnishings — including kitchen accessories, dinnerware, glassware, and metal ware — while the others accepted commissions to work as well on appliances, machines, and other industrial items. With the aim of providing reasonably-priced, well-designed accessories to enhance the informal lifestyles of most middle-class Americans, Wright also was less of a social reformer than some other industrial designers.

He first turned to the production of dinnerware in the 1930s, after he had decided that most dishes being manufactured at the time did not enhance the appearance of the food served on them. After investigating, with the aid of photographic studies, a variety of dish shapes and hues in relation to the specific foods placed on them, Wright came up with the design for the informal *American Modern* dinnerware. The 1937 design was revolutionary for the times, with its sculptural organic rimless forms and its unusual mottled hues such as Bean Brown, Sea Foam Blue, Chartreuse Curry and Granite Gray. These were the colors that Wright had determined by experiment as making food appear at its most aesthetically pleasing. Another innovation introduced by Wright with *American Modern* was that the dinnerware settings could be used in combinations of colors — with, for instance, a plate of one color matched up with a bowl, saucer and cup, each of a different color.

The simplified flowing shapes developed by Wright for *American Modern* dinnerware and its accompanying serving pieces bore a close resemblance to the aerodynamic streamlined form promoted by the industrial designers of the 1930s. According to Wright, this was not his intent. Apparently, he had colonial American prototypes in mind for *American Modern*; the shape of the water pitcher was suggested by that of the traditional American coalscuttle, while the soup bowls were inspired by eighteenth century porringers. But the affinity of *American Modern* — particularly of its creamers, teapots, and pitchers — for the teardrop-shaped ideal of the streamlined movement was unmistakable. This conclusion is reinforced by the eventual widespread success of Wright's design during an era whose decorative arts were dominated by the streamlined style.

Nevertheless, success did not come easily. For two years a number of New York department stores and dishware manufacturers refused to produce Wright's line, because they feared that it was too avant-garde for depression times. Ohio's Steubenville Pottery finally agreed to manufacture *American Modern* on the condition that Wright himself finance production costs. After the china was produced, Wright then had to struggle to overcome the resistance of department store buyers. In desperation, he pioneered the concept of 'starter sets' that could be sold at close to cost, in the expectation that the customers would decide to complete their sets with the far more expensive service pieces.

Success, when it finally came, was phenomenal. Wright's name rapidly became a household word, as over 80 million pieces of the china were made between 1939 and 1959. At first, before Steubenville Pottery doubled its size, *American Modern* was in such demand that shipments arriving at stores required police to maintain order among the frenzied waiting customers. *American Modern* may well have been the most popular mass-produced dinnerware line ever sold.

But the appeal of *American Modern* dinnerware was probably based more on its modernistic style, than on its actual functional superiority. The flowing shapes were fragile, tending to chip and break rather easily. And the small cup handles were difficult for large hands to hold; also, the rimless plates allowed food to spill easily. In these respects the more traditional shapes that had evolved through centuries of usage were, in reality, more functional than *American Modern*. This paradox was not unfamiliar to modern design. When Wright redesigned *American Modern* for institutional use in 1948, he tried to correct some of these drawbacks by using heavier duty vitreous china and by making the shapes less freeform. The restaurant *American Modern* dinnerware was also made available in a wider range of colors, among them Straw Yellow.

The success of *American Modern* dinnerware was probably a significant factor in the creation of Castleton Museum White dinnerware, the result of a collaboration between Castleton China Company and the Museum of Modern Art. The museum's endorsement on a product of advanced modern design was certain, according to company thinking, to ensure a profitable product. The dinnerware was developed under the museum's aegis by Hungarian immigrant Eva Zeisel, who then taught design at New York's Pratt Institute. The design of Castleton Museum White was completed over the years 1941 to 1943; and the result was simple, flowing and pure white, with predetermined variations in thickness. The general impression was of a dinnerware not so very far removed from Russel Wright's concept for *American Modern*; Wright's varied colors, however, were abandoned in favor of the white preferred by practitioners of the Bauhaus-influenced International Style.

Production difficulties were caused by the variations in thickness, and by the fact that the pristine white surface

showed the slightest flaw. But after a 1946 Museum of Modern Art exhibition, Castleton Museum White dinnerware sold relatively well to those members of the general public who appreciated modern design.

Probably the most typical and most widely available art deco dinnerwares available from the mid 1930s on were the mass-produced Fiesta and Harlequin lines, both made by West Virginia's Homer Laughlin Company. Fiesta ware began production in 1936 and some items continued to be made well into the 1960s. Harlequin ware, intended as a less expensive version of Fiesta and sold exclusively in Woolworth stores, was first issued in 1938 and was also produced into the 1960s. In celebration of Woolworth's 100th anniversary in the 1970s, Harlequin ware was reissued for a limited period of time.

The names, Fiesta and Harlequin, referred to the wide range of bright colors in which these dishes appeared. As with Russel Wright's *American Modern*, customers were encouraged to mix colors within place settings. The vivid hues of the dishes probably helped to serve as a visual antidote to the general gloom of the depression era. Both dishware lines were characterized by the angular geometric shapes of their cups, bowls, and other vertical containers. All of these items, including the plates, typically bore a decorative motif of incised concentric circles, or parallel encircling lines. These were similar to the designs of some art deco glassware, which had been produced earlier than and during the same years as Fiesta and Harlequin ware.

The dramatic conical shapes of items as the cups and shakers reflected cubist prototypes of the 1920s, while the bands of parallel lines and concentric circles were allied to streamlined design motifs of the 1930s. Harlequin ware items, such as the salt and pepper shakers, tended to be more elongated and more sharply angled than Fiesta ware. Also, in Harlequin ware, the band of evenly spaced rings began farther from the rim of the vessel. The more costly Fiesta was also more subtly refined than the Harlequin ware — in the Fiesta, the concentric rings, which extended to the edge of the plate, were gradually spaced more widely as they approached the rim; and some Fiesta items such as tumblers frequently incorporated a slightly flared effect in the sides of the vessel, while similar Harlequin articles had straight angled sides.

During the 1930s and subsequent years, a number of other inexpensive heavier-bodied, less well-documented ceramic vessels, the most attractive of which were the bowls and pitchers, were also produced. Their similarly vivid colors, and volumetric shapes and ornament — which included incised lines in geometric or circular patterns, or in parallel stripes — marked their art deco influence. During the World War II years, a number of these items were sometimes given away, as were Harlequin and Fiesta ware, as premiums with refrigerators or other major appliance or furniture purchases. In any case such art deco derived ceramic wares generally became available in stores nationwide, as the more elite examples of art deco style created by the art potters and by the more cosmopolitan urban-based designers eventually diffused throughout the country in a more conservative, but still unmistakable art deco form.

Glass

Glassware was another realm of the decorative arts that reflected art deco tendencies. The most characteristic American art deco glass items were produced by concerns catering to opposite ends of the consumer market. Steuben Glass produced exquisite costly limited edition art objects that bore images and patterns strongly indebted to the French floral, animal and figural designs displayed at the 1925 Paris exposition. During the same years, various considerably less elite companies – including Diamond Glassware, Hazel Atlas Glass, Hocking Glass, Indiana Glass, Jeannette Glass and a division of Corning (Steuben's parent company) – produced a limited number of more avant-garde and much less costly art deco dinnerware designs based on cubist and streamlined motifs.

In general, as was the case with residential architecture of the twenties and thirties, most of the designs produced by glassmakers were recreations of historical styles – particularly popular were the revivals of renaissance and of American colonial era styles. The participants in the industrial design movement of the thirties also produced a body of glassware that was less overtly art deco, and was more allied to Bauhaus-derived ideas of simple and functional design as seen, for instance, in utilitarian items for the home that were based on laboratory glass designs.

Steuben Glass was a relative newcomer to the glass industry. Founded in 1903 by Englishman Frederick Carder and named after American Revolutionary War hero Baron von Steuben and after Corning's site in Steuben County, New York, Steuben Glass originally was organized to produce raw crystal blanks for Corning glasscutters. Steuben became a division of Corning in 1918. Carder's great artistic abilities led to the creation of a line of colored art glass, much of it in the art nouveau style, that was produced until 1933. Many of the early generation of Steuben craftsmen, both glassmakers and engravers, were trained in traditional European centers of glassmaking – Austria, Czechoslovakia, England, Germany and Sweden.

Under Frederick Carder, the colored art glass, particularly in the years preceding World War I, continued European design traditions. Carder himself was the designer of many of the finest items, and he was quick to follow contemporary trends. His gold aurene vase with an art deco design of patterned foliage was of the type popular in the twenties and that continued to be made into the thirties. The vase was of encased glass, with a darker layer bearing the acid-etched decoration covering a

Below: Frederick Carder, hunting pattern vase, Steuben, circa 1925.
Below right: F Carder, Winton pattern vase, Steuben, circa 1932.

thinner inner layer. Another elegant vase – one of acid cut translucent red glass, decorated with a 'hunting' pattern – underlined Carder's debt to French art deco designers. The leaping gazelle, the dramatically stylized foliage and landscape, and the rhythmic curves and zigzags were motifs frequently applied to European works.

The great depression brought hard times to Steuben Glass, just as it did to many other companies. In an attempt to revive the faltering concern, Carder was replaced in 1933 as head of Steuben by Arthur A Houghton, Jr, whose family owned Corning Glass. Houghton immediately implemented radical policy changes. The colored glass line was completely eliminated; and henceforth Steuben was to produce only items of colorless pure crystal, with an emphasis on harmony between the swelling fluid forms of the massive vessels and their engraved designs. This glass, based on a new formulation, originally had been developed for technological application but had proven too soft for such use. This industrial mishap was exploited by Houghton who, in short order, was able to raise Steuben's glass objects to a fine art status by hiring designers of the level of Sidney Waugh, an American sculptor and 1929 Prix de Rome winner.

Now in the collections of major museums in the United States and abroad, Waugh's first design for Steuben was executed as the 1935 *Gazelle Bowl*. The frieze of twelve stylized leaping gazelles was a restatement of a motif popular to the twenties that was seen not only in French design, but also in the sculpture of Paul Manship, in ceramics and sculpture by W Hunt Diederich, and even in advertising illustrations for newspapers and magazines. Yet, the understated, unornamented parallel paired lines above and below the gazelles reflected the 1930s streamlined style motif of speed stripes; and the massive quality of the bowl and its base echoed cubist interests in geometry in mass, as well as current developments in architecture – specifically the monumentalism preferred for the classical moderne buildings, erected by the New Deal Public Works Administration. This bowl was first engraved by master craftsman, Hungarian-born Joseph Libisch, who had trained in Vienna and Prague, and had entered Steuben employ in 1921. Libisch subsequently trained many other Steuben engravers.

The *Zodiac Bowl*, also designed in 1935 by Sidney Waugh and again first engraved by Libisch, depicted another omnipresent motif of the late twenties. Astrological imagery was frequently used in the ornate lobby decor of buildings in the zigzag style. And the sun motif was yet another popular art deco motif of those years. The idealized heroic figures decorating the bowl were similar to the classically-derived figures so often seen in the relief sculptures and murals decorating many of the New Deal PWA buildings.

As its international reputation increased to equal those of such European glass producers as Baccarat and Lalique of France and Orrefors of Sweden, Steuben was able to commission a group of 27 foremost American and European painters and sculptors to create designs to be engraved on glass in 1937. In the same year, Steuben received the gold medal at the Paris exposition. Steuben pieces were subsequently exhibited at the 1939 San

Above: Carder continued art nouveau lines in the art deco era.

Francisco and New York expositions, as well as in major American museums.

This development of an elite image for Steuben glass undoubtedly was reinforced by Houghton's innovative marketing strategy which made Steuben objects less accessible to the general public. During the earlier Carder era, Steuben glass had been sold indiscriminately in a wide range of stores, but in 1933 Houghton decided to sell Steuben glass items only in specialized Steuben shops, situated on New York's Fifth Avenue and later in other major cities.

Nevertheless, the general American populace was also in a position to obtain glass items in art deco designs. During the twenties and thirties, a kind of inexpensive glassware now known as Depression glass was widely manufactured. Produced in a variety of colors and decorative patterns, the molded and totally machine-made glass was produced mainly in the form of utilitarian household and restaurant dishes, bowls, cups, glasses, pitchers, candy dishes and various other serving pieces. The majority of the Depression glass designs were based on traditional patterns, such as Sandwich glass, in which the design was etched into the mold, paralleling the effect of the much more expensive acid etching. Other molds

gave the effect of cut glass. A limited number of art deco patterns were also made, and these modernist lines were primarily dynamic treatments of cubist and streamlined motifs.

Depression glass was usually manufactured of the cheapest kind of commercial glass, and the colors – most frequently pastel green, yellow and pink, though eventually all hues, including crystal or clear glass, were made – served to disguise flaws in the glass. But despite the poor finishing of and impurities in individual items, Depression glass, of which the smaller items cost three or four cents each, sold widely. It was, in fact much cheaper than ceramic dishware and during hard economic times, cost rather than quality was a primary consideration for the majority of Americans. The variety of attractive patterns and colors available made the glassware a desirable purchase for many households.

Depression glass also became an essential part of the marketing strategy of using premiums to promote other products and services. A number of movie theaters, for example, had 'dish nights' on which customers could receive free glassware items; while some furniture stores would give away complete sets of Depression glass with the purchase of a dining room or living room suite, or of a major appliance.

While most Depression wares appeared in the form of

translucent colored glass, some of the items were also produced in more costly opaque form – desirable to those no doubt, who valued its resemblance to regular ceramic dishware, or perhaps its reported heat resistant qualities. Notable among the opaque varieties appearing in art deco designs was the Ovide line produced from 1930 to 1935 by Hazel Atlas Glass Company. The Platonite, as the manufacturer called it, had a fired on colored design strongly reminiscent of the china designed by Frank Lloyd Wright for Tokyo's Imperial Hotel, although in the Depression ware the skyscraper motif supplemented the circular pattern. The shapes of the various Ovide plates and vessels remained relatively traditional. Opaque glassware, in more modernistic shapes, some of which had a marbled coloristic effect, were produced from 1913 to 1951 by Akro Agate Company.

The cubist influence was most quintessentially apparent in Indiana Glass Company's Number 610 – renamed 'Pyramid' by recent collectors – manufactured from 1926 to 1932. Here the exaggerated conical shapes of the pitchers and glasses, the abrupt angles of the handles, and the jagged silhouette of the molded design aptly translated the zigzag patterns of the skyscraper style. In practice, glass was more adaptable than ceramics to such angular shapes and patterns; similar cubist effects could be produced in ceramics only through the use of applied decoration.

Also cubist in design was Jeannette Glass Company's Sierra pattern (1931-1933), which was only produced for a short while, as the pinwheel design was stylish but highly

Left: Sidney Waugh, *Gazelle Bowl*, 1935, Steuben Glass.
Below: Ovide pattern, Hazel Atlas Glass Co, 1930-35.

Left: Pyramid pattern, Indiana Glass Co., 1926-32.
Below left: Manhattan pattern, Anchor Hocking Glass Co, 1938-41.

impractical. The serrated projecting edges chipped very easily. A more durable version of cubist-derived art deco ware was made by Indiana Glass Company in a heavier glass from 1926 to 1931. Known as 'Tea Room,' this glassware was meant primarily for the commercial tea rooms and ice cream parlors of the day. It could also be purchased for home use, as with the increasing general availability of domestic electric refrigerators, people could enjoy more frequently such pleasures as ice cream at home. In the Tea Room pattern, the dynamic geometric shapes of the ridged and graduated block optic design appeared in such speciality items as banana split bowls, sherbert dishes, footed sundae dishes, and ice buckets, as well as candlesticks and even lamps. Thus the commercial establishment setting its tables with Tea Room glassware could also purchase matching lighting fixtures to achieve the unity of design so important to the art deco era.

The dominant thirties streamlined style also inspired the design of various Depression glass lines. Streamlined curved forms and speed stripes appeared in various patterns manufactured by Hocking Glass during the 1930s. Among them were 'Ring,' 'Circle' and most notably 'Manhattan.' Also known as 'Horizontal Ribbed,' Manhattan was made from 1938 to 1941. It was a simple but dramatic and futuristic-looking design that was probably most effective in crystal, or clear glass, although it was also available in pastel pink and green. From 1934 to 1942, Hazel Atlas Glass Company produced a pattern similar in spirit. In 'Moderntone,' the concentric ring pattern was flatter than that of Manhattan, and the handles of its cups and pitchers were more angular, like those of the cubist-derived designs. A unique feature of Moderntone was the pairing of many of its serving dishes with hemispherical chrome-plated lids. This combination was particularly effective when the glass hue was cobalt blue, or Ritz Blue, as it was then named – the Moderntone punch bowl set was a striking example. The glass companies vied to produce such items, as well as cocktail shakers, decanters, ice buckets and glasses to mark the repeal of Prohibition. Before repeal, such alcohol related items were advertised with the stated function of serving 'grape juice.'

The Depression glass companies made traditional and art deco designs available to the largest possible audience. This democratizing trend was quite the opposite from the intentions of Steuben Glass, which managed to survive and indeed thrive throughout the depression decade by making its products available, by reason of cost and inaccessibility, to only a wealthy few. Depression glass had further social significance in the ways in which it reflected changes in American life during the decades between the two world wars. In those years, the general availability of the new electric refrigerators led the glass manufacturers to produce new kinds of items to be used in conjunction with these appliances. Among them were covered butter dishes, refrigerator storage boxes, water carafes, ice tubs and tilt jugs. The new refrigerated railroad cars brought fresh oranges to the colder states, and the resulting taste for fresh orange juice led to the production of Depression

Above: Sidney Waugh, *Zodiac Bowl*, 1935, Steuben Glass.

glass reamers to squeeze the oranges. And new ideas about the importance of a balanced diet led to the production of compartmented dinner dishes, also known as grill plates. (Perhaps another consideration in the design of such plates was that smaller servings of food in depression-era America seemed larger on such divided dishes.) Similar compartmented plates were available in the ceramic dinnerware lines of Harlequin and Fiesta. Depression glass dishes were widely purchased and used during the 1920s and 1930s, and their low cost undercut that of ceramic dinnerware. As a result many ceramic dish producers went out of business during the thirties, while the glassware companies flourished.

Below: Tea Room plate, Indiana Glass Co., 1926-31.

Metalware

The style-conscious American buying public had already been exposed to the finest examples of European design in metal serving dishes and flatware well before the 1925 Paris exposition. The work of Georg Jensen, an internationally respected Danish silversmith, had been displayed at the 1915 Panama-Pacific Exposition in San Francisco and newspaper magnate William Randolph Hearst had purchased most of the Jensen silver on view there. In 1923, Jensen opened a New York City store, and his simple, solid forms became a pervasive influence on American silversmiths. At the same time, French designs by Jean Puiforcat and others had been available in Manhattan's leading department stores from the early 1920s on.

American manufacturing companies soon began to make their own mass-produced art deco designs available at moderate cost. International Silver Company of Meriden, Connecticut, introduced its 'Northern Lights' pattern with a linear stylized wave design around the base of the bowl, reportedly adapted by a motif from illustrator Rockwell Kent. In 1934 International Silver first offered signed pieces by designer Lurelle Guild; his bowls, covered dishes, and wine coolers were ornamented with streamlined stripes.

Other American produced art deco metalware was designed by European-trained craftsmen. Denmark's Erik

Above: International Silver Co, 'Ebb Tide' bowl and 'Northern Lights' underplate, circa 1928.

Magnussen was left free to experiment with modernist ideas by Gorham Manufacturing Company, for whom he worked from 1925 to 1929. His 1929 avant garde coffee service, 'The Lights and Shadows of Manhattan,' with its faceted reflective surfaces was based on cubist themes. More conservative interpretations of cubist ideas in metalware were produced by a number of designers. Among them was Hungarian born and trained illustrator and designer Ilonka Karasz, whose 1929 tea set was typical of such work. The restrained shapes of her vessels were based on the cubist inspired geometry of the cone

Below: Erik Magnussen, 'The Lights and Shadows of Manhattan' coffee service, Gorham Manufacturing Co, 1927.

and cylinder; and the exaggerated rectangular handle silhouettes and the sharp angular spouts, along with the stepped-back lids, possessed a functional simplicity closely allied to Bauhaus designs, as well as to the French works of Puiforcat and Donald Desny. Cubist-inspired tea and coffee services by other designers working in America had pots in rectangular and even trapezoidal shapes with exaggerated angular or curved handles.

Following his credo that rejected historical styles, Eliel Saarinen also produced a number of designs for metal serving vessels and flatware between 1928 and 1931. International Silver Company fabricated some of Saarinen's prototypes for the 1929 and 1934 Metropolitan Museum of Art exhibitions, but the company actually sold only one item commercially – a flat silver centerpiece with a round foot. A number of Saarinen's designs for flatware incorporated art deco motifs. A 1931 design for a short-bladed knife had a geometric setback pattern for the handle, reflecting the then current skyscraper style, while a 1934 silver urn, in its simple volumetric form, had an affinity with the cubist geometry of the sphere and cylinder. With its rejection of surface decoration, the urn celebrated, in its gleaming purity, the machine aesthetic which was so central to art deco. Incidentally, the versatile Saarinen had also designed ceramic dishes for the same 1929 Metropolitan Museum exhibition. Made by Lenox, his porcelain dinner service with its angular shapes and linear geometric pattern reflected an earlier design by Josef Hoffmann of the Wiener Werkatätte, and echoed as well his own side chairs for his room in the Metropolitan exhibition.

Harry Bertoia, who in 1937 assumed the direction of the Cranbrook Academy silver and metal working studio, designed and produced a number of silver coffee and tea services, also based on cubist design principles, during his earlier years there. A 1940 set had dramatic arc-shaped handles of cherrywood and volumetric vessels with their sides sliced by sudden parabolic curves. Bertoia also produced other 'jazzy' sets in this spirit with lucite handles.

The machine aesthetic was even more thoroughly exploited by Chase Brass and Copper Company of Waterbury, Connecticut, originally a producer of tubing, pipe and industrial wire. Chase's moderately priced chromium household accessories lines, initiated in 1930, included items such as smoking and drinking-related specialty items, as well as ornamental objects such as candlesticks, bud vases and more traditional coffee services. Most of these designs, of combined geometric forms, were fabricated from standard widths of industrial pipe and sheet metal. Many of these items also included some art deco style striping or similar detail. Designer Walter von Nessen's 'Diplomat' coffee service for Chase was innovatively constructed from extruded chromium plated pipe, while its vertical fluted styling and ebony-like black plastic handles gave it the aura of Viennese elegance.

In 1937, Revere Copper and Brass Company hired industrial designer Norman Bel Geddes to create a 'Skyscraper' cocktail shaker and a 'Manhattan' serving tray edged with architecturally inspired setbacks. This continuation of 1920s style art deco motifs well into the streamlined era possibly suggests a nostalgic longing for

Above: Copper candlestick designed by Reimann, Chase Brass & Copper Co, 1931-41.

the frivolous and prosperous twenties from the austere perspective of the depression-era thirties. Industrial, furniture and interior designer Kem Weber also produced modernistic designs inspired by the machine aesthetic for silver cocktail shakers, vases and other items for New York's Friedman Silver Company in 1928.

As were many other designers of the era, Russel Wright was deeply involved in the exploration of new materials and processes in order to provide aesthetic pleasure and appropriate function to the consumer at reasonable cost. In the early 1930s, Wright began to experiment with chrome-plated steel and spun pewter made into bar accessories such as glasses, bowls and cocktail shakers in the form of gleaming cylindrical and spherical industrially inspired shapes. But the necessity for special plating and fabricating machinery for such items attracted Wright instead to the more easily worked aluminum which, spun and abraded with emery cloth, resembled pewter. Wright's spun aluminum line, designed in exaggerated shapes, was so successful that he widened his range of serving pieces to include trays, soup tureens, ice buckets, stove-to-table wares and other vessels. Thus, middle-class Americans were able to purchase modern design objects specifically geared to their more informal life style.

Left: Walter von Nessen, coffee set, The Chase Brass & Copper Co.
Above: Ilonka Karasz, tea set, 1929.
Below: Candlesticks manufactured by The Chase Brass & Copper Co.

Plastics

Just as the experimentation with unusual metallic materials such as aluminum and chrome was important in the household accessories industry, so did the recently invented synthetic material of plastic become an object of design focus. Several types of plastics, partially derived from natural raw materials, already had been formulated during the later part of the nineteenth century. Among them were vulcanite (a combination of rubber and sulphur), celluloid (often used for imitation tortoise shell and ivory ornaments), cellulose acetate (used for photographic film, knife handles and pen barrels) and casein (used for buttons).

In 1907 Belgian chemist Leo Baekland developed the first completely synthetic resin, phenol formaldehyde, popularly known as bakelite, for use as electrical insulation. The versatility of bakelite soon led to its wide application in industrial design and the decorative arts.

Its hardness and resemblance to wood saw bakelite molded into a variety of shapes – for radio cabinets, pot handles, knobs, automobile dashboards and incorporated as well into fine furniture in the art deco style. Bakelite was also used in colorful art deco powder compacts, cigarette boxes and desk accessories. It was molded into jewelry, hair ornaments, and hat and shoe clips. Some of these plastic ornaments were intended as imitations of natural materials such as coral, agate, ivory, tortoise shell, mother of pearl or jade; while other jewelry and ornaments were designed in chunky cubist derived forms with molded stylized decoration that appeared to be carved. Many of these latter ornaments did not try to resemble more costly materials, but were instead colorfully and proudly what they were – pure plastic.

Right: The Fada radio, drink mixers and bangle bracelets, **(above)**, and the bracelet and pin, **(below)**, were made of colourful plastic.

6
INDUSTRIAL DESIGN

A major source of design ideas for the streamlined phase of art deco were the industrial designers who rose to prominence during the 1930s. As a profession, industrial design – in the form of freelance consultants – was a new phenomenon tied to the marketing needs of American manufacturers who were under urgent pressure to stimulate adequate consumer interest in their products during the economically depressed era. During the height of 1920s prosperity, many industrial concerns initiated ambitious expansion programs, with the result that the supply of manufactured products soon threatened to far exceed actual consumer demand. The ensuing fierce competition for the customer dollar placed new emphasis on stylish repackaging of the whole range of available mass produced items, from railroad trains to pencil sharpeners, and including in between such items as automobiles, office equipment, household appliances, furniture, radios and camera. Attention was also focused on optimal methods of promoting sales, and hence resulted in the modernistic transformation of such heretofore traditional sales outlets as advertising, store window displays and commercial interiors.

Few of those who became industrial designers were trained professionally either as engineers or as architects. Rather, they predominantly came from the field of advertising and commercial illustration, as did Walter Dorwin Teague, Raymond Loewy, Lurelle Guild, George Sakier, Egmont Arens, Joseph Sinel and George Switzer – or from the field of stage design, as did Norman Bel Geddes, Henry Dreyfuss, John Vassos and Russel Wright. Many of the prominent designers were immigrants, among them William Lescaze (also an influential architect), Raymond Loewy, Frederick Kiesler, Otto Kuhler, Gustav Jensen, Joseph Sinel, Kem Weber and Peter Muller Munk, while some of the native-born Americans had studied in Europe. Indeed, a number of the industrial designers originally had studied painting and other fine arts. This

Left: RCA Victor Model TRK-9 Television Receiver, 1939.
Right: Joseph Sinel, skyscraper style scale for International Ticket Scale Corporation.

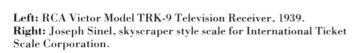

conjunction of artistic and industrial interests was not unique to twentieth century Americans. During the nineteenth century, two painters had been pivotal inventors, Robert Fulton of the first operable steamboat, and Samuel Morse of the telegraph.

Most of the industrial designers were remarkably versatile in the projects they tackled, although some remained relatively specialized. Donald Deskey, Gilbert Rohde, Kem Weber and Russel Wright concentrated on the design of mass-produced furniture and household accessories, while others such as Otto Kuhler concentrated on the design of transportation vehicles. In general the industrial design movement was centered on the east coast, in and around New York City, but there were also a few designers who carried on successful careers elsewhere, as did Harold Van Doren in Ohio and Kem Weber in California. And while most designers functioned as freelance consultants, there were also those who became

Left: Fada Radio. Radios were continually restyled in the 1930s.
Below: Patriot Radio and assorted canisters.
Right above: Harlequin baking dish; Fiesta demitasse and saucer.
Right below: Shelf clock, Manning Bowman & Co, circa 1928-31.

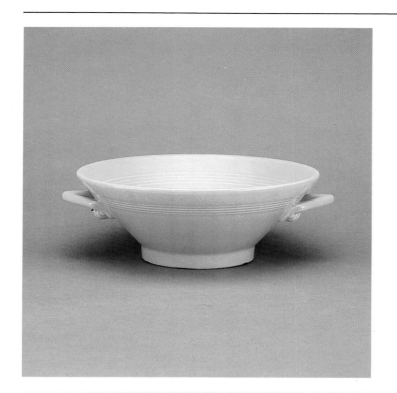

in-house designers for large corporations; among these were George Sakier at American Radiator, Donald Dohner at Westinghouse, and Ray Patten at General Electric.

The dramatic rise of the industrial design profession owed much to earlier developments. Since the late 19th century, American mass-produced goods had an abysmally poor reputation. The then influential Arts and Crafts Movement sought to raise the level of American goods by promoting well-designed high-quality hand work over the ubiquitous shoddy machine made products. This prevailing view was countered by Frank Lloyd Wright in a 1901 speech in which he raised the future possibility of using machines to produce well-designed and well-made household furnishings. America was not yet ready for such a revolutionary proposal, but Wright's ideas were more eagerly received in Europe.

In 1907, the Deutscher Werkbund was founded in Germany, with an invitational membership of architects, designers, and manufacturers, to counter negative attitudes toward the machine and to attempt to apply aesthetic principles in a collaborative way to the design of machine-made goods. The Werkbund was succeeded in

Left: Santa Fe Railway's El Capitan, a streamlined coach train.
Below: Kem Weber, tubular steel furniture designs, 1934, for Lloyd Manufacturing Company, Menominee, Michigan.

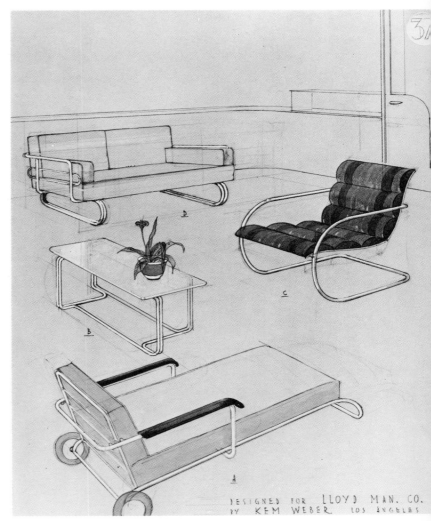

1919 by the Bauhaus, a German design school whose curriculum of fine and applied arts endorsed a pure functionalist aesthetic. Bauhaus ideas had a profound influence on American design, particularly after the rise of Nazism resulted in the emigration of several key members, including Walter Gropius, Mies van der Rohe, Josef Albers and Laszlo Moholy-Nagy, to the United States during the 1930s.

As the machine aesthetic became an important feature of avant-garde art, another key event was the 1923 publication by French-Swiss painter and architect Le Corbusier of *Vers une Architecture (Towards a New Architecture)*. In this seminal book, Le Corbusier promoted the idea of the house as a 'machine for living,' praised the mass production assembly line techniques first introduced in 1913 by Henry Ford, and saw the development of the airplane as a logical engineering model for the solution of other design and social problems of the modern age. The beauty of the machine and its concomitant efficiency hence were elevated as universal values.

Streamlining came to be the style almost universally applied by the American industrial designers of the 1930s. With its flowing curved lines and aerodynamic form, the streamlined style symbolically suggested efficiency and speed, an effect enhanced by the addition of parallel horizontal speed stripes on smooth gleaming, often

Left: A Greyhound Bus Depot in Columbia, South Carolina.
Right: A typical streamlined tropical art deco building in Florida's old Miami Beach section.
Below: Gordon M Buehrig, designer, Cord 810 Phaeton, 1936, built by Auburn Automobile Company.

Left and above: Santa Fe Railway's *Super Chief* Acoma lounge combined streamlining, exotic veneers and Pueblo deco, 1937.

metallic, surfaces. Streamlining ostensibly derived from the airplane but its curves were already apparent, in the years when airplanes were still angular, in the designs of German architect Eric Mendelsohn, in World War I era dirigibles, and in some later Deutscher Werkbund locomotive designs.

The chief promoter of the streamlined style in the United States was stage designer Norman Bel Geddes, who had established an industrial design firm in 1927. Geddes seemed little more than a visionary dreamer, but his

Below: Santa Fe Super Chief observation lounge car.

Above: New York Central's super train, the Twentieth Century Limited. Designer Henry Dreyfuss restyled the locomotive.

fantastic designs for colossal luxury airplanes, svelte streamlined ocean liners and the 'ultimate car' illustrated in his persuasive book, *Horizons*, proved remarkably successful in popularizing the style. Geddes' more outlandish ideas remained unrealized, but his firm did produce designs for stoves, radios and airplane interiors. At the end of the decade, his utopian fervor was granted a forum at the 1939 New York World's Fair, particularly in the General Motors Futurama display, 'City of Tomorrow.'

A fellow visionary was R Buckminster Fuller. His six-sided 1929 Dymaxion House, intended for mass production, and his streamlined designs for the three-wheeled Dymaxion Car (1927-1934) and for prefabricated one-piece stainless steel bathroom units (1937) never progressed beyond the prototype stage. Fame came to Fuller only in later decades, with the practical applications of his geodesic dome.

French-born Raymond Loewy was another flamboyant exponent of streamlining. Although he was best known for his transportation vehicle designs, particularly the Greyhound buses, trucks and locomotives, he also produced progressively more aerodynamic designs for such diverse products as Sears Coldspot refrigerators, International Harvester cream separators and a controversial pencil sharpener. Loewy's designs for streamlined automobiles,

notably the Hupmobile, were less successful. It remained to designer Gordon Buehrig to produce the masterpiece of American streamlined automobile styling – the 1936 Cord.

During the middle of the decade, the industrial designers enlarged their field of activity to include store interiors, commercial showrooms, and especially train and airplane interiors. The prototype for a sleek industrial designer's office created by Loewy in association with Lee Simonson for the 1934 Metropolitan Museum industrial art exhibit conveyed, with its streamlined window and speed striped walls, the ultimate in modern efficiency. Similarly streamlined interiors were designed for trains and planes. Occasionally an anachronistic taste for 1920s opulence resulted in such hybrid streamlined zigzag moderne train interiors such as the exotic pueblo deco ornament, accompanied by richly veneered exotic woods, in the Acoma Super Chief. Nor were all appliances streamlined. That the now outdated zigzag style was still appreciated by some more conservative clients could be seen in Joseph Sinel's skyscraper style scale, and in speed striped skyscraper style plastic radios designed by Harold Van Doren and John Gordon Rideout.

Henry Dreyfuss was relatively unique among the industrial designers in his sensitivity to the particular needs of each client and for going beyond surface style to create designs suitable to each individual product. This approach did not appeal to all manufacturers, but Dreyfuss nevertheless had notable successes with such projects as

Above: A streamlined gas station in New Orleans, Louisiana.
Left: Walter Dorwin Teague, Kodak Bantam Special camera, 1936-37.

his locomotive designs for New York Central's Mercury and the Twentieth Century Limited, as well as the 1937 Bell Telephone desk model and his series of Big Ben alarm clocks.

Walter Dorwin Teague had a similarly pragmatic approach to design. His attention to manufacturers' needs and production techniques led to such continuing commissions as a 30-year association as design consultant to Eastman Kodak. Teague's elegant design for the 1936 Kodak Bantam Special camera epitomized the application of streamlined styling to small appliances. Teague also left his mark on the design of tractors, x-ray machines, air conditioning equipment, and a series of streamlined gas stations for Texaco. He held strongly felt utopian convictions in the belief that good design had wider implications in social engineering and eventually could lead to a better future for all. These ideals culminated in his work on the futuristic exhibits at the New York World's Fair.

Such a characteristic invention of the modern age as the radio was continually restyled by its manufacturers. The individualistic Russel Wright resisted the extreme application of the streamlined style in his 1932 table model for Wurlitzer, but still acknowledged its influence in the subtly rounded corners, the striping and curving in the speaker-dial grouping, and the smooth uncluttered surfaces. RCA Victor's 1939 pioneer television was encased in

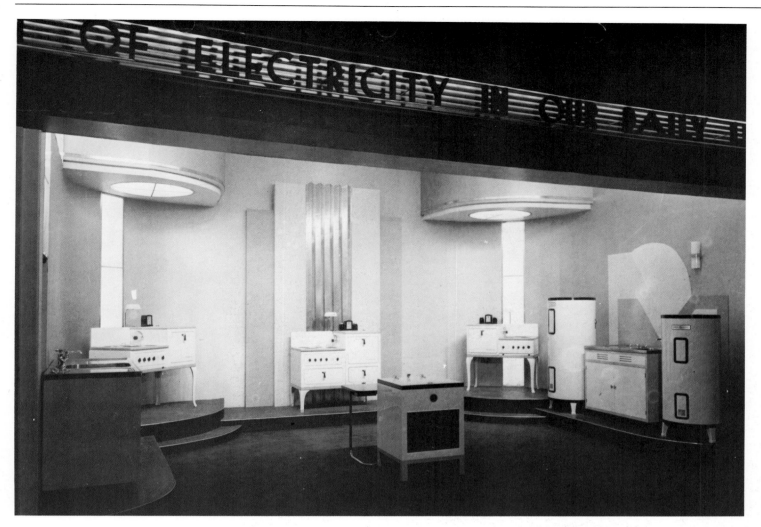

Left: Wurlitzer juke box, circa 1946.
Above: This 1933 Chicago fair display setting was streamlined, but similar restyling still lay ahead for the GE appliances.
Right: Russel Wright, Lyric table radio, Wurlitzer Co, 1932.

a more traditionally oriented cabinet combining the curves and stripes of the streamlined style with the dramatic contrast of dark wood grains seen in French-influenced 1920s art deco style furniture. And juke boxes maintained their hybrid and appropriately kitschy art deco ostentation well into the following decades.

Streamlining, despites its highly promoted functionalism, was in effect a surface veneer – a repackaging in a modernistic shell of the unwieldy and frequently unaltered machine parts underneath. The style's main function was to attract new customers by means of its persuasive allusions to modernism, high style, efficiency, and speed. Certainly, there was a seductive degree of logic to the latter implications in such streamlined appliances as vacuum cleaners and washing machines, but the logic was more tenuous in relation to such items as stoves and refrigerators. It has been suggested that the style's symbolic allusions also had broader implications. The attempt to streamline the complete man-made environment during the 1930s was appealing because it optimistically suggested the nation's ability to move forward – decisively, quickly, and with little friction – leaving behind forever the chaotic social realities of the depression years.

7
NEW DEAL ART PROGRAMS

An unprecedented and vast experiment in the governmental patronage of the arts was initiated by the New Deal programs of the Roosevelt administration in an effort to alleviate unemployment during the depression years. The several involved agencies – the 1933-1934 Public Works of Art Project (PWAP); the 1934 Section of Painting and Sculpture (SPS) of the Treasury Department, which in 1938 was renamed the Treasury Section of Fine Arts, and in 1939 became known as the Public Buildings Administration; and the 1935-1943 Federal Art Project (FAP)

Left: Detail of Maxine Albro's 1934 mural, *California Agriculture*, for San Francisco's Coit Tower.
Below: Omaha Union Station, dining room mural, 1929-30. Railways pioneered such mural decoration of public facilities.

which operated under the auspices of the Works Progress Administration (WPA) – kept thousands of artists, designers and architects at work during the 1930s.

The older generation of involved artists included many who had created art deco and related works. Indeed, a number of these artists were chosen for administrative positions in the New Deal art agencies. And a number of the then lesser known artists – including Philip Guston, Lee Krasner, Jackson Pollock, Arshile Gorky, Willem de Kooning, Ilya Bolotowsky, David Smith, and Louise Nevelson – went on to become the stars of the post-World War II era.

Because of the conservatism of popular taste, particularly in the rural areas, abstract art was overwhelmingly overshadowed in the New Deal works by stylized repre-

Above: Daniel Celentano, *Commerce*, 1936, for Queens library.

sentational imagery which incorporated many of the art deco motifs dealing with transportation, communications, dynamic energy, and mythologized heroic human figures. The art deco influence was most apparent in the murals and the relief sculpture that adorned so much of the New Deal classical moderne architecture. The hard-edged, relief-like art deco style was also appropriate in that it was more visible in less than ideally lit interiors. Many of the New Deal graphic works also owed a debt to art deco.

By far the most controversial of the government sponsored art works were the murals painted in post offices, hospitals, schools, libraries, civic structures, courthouses, prisons, air terminals and other public buildings nationwide. Even though the individual mural designs

were selected by national and regional juries, the discord at the mural site frequently was intense and centered on local criticisms of dreary portrayals, nudism, and inappropriate political content. The preferred murals were upbeat; depicted dignified, attractive and fully clothed characters; and showed inspiring incidents from local or national history. Local dissension was also roused by the fact that bureaucratic authorities in far away Washington decided precisely what images were to be installed in small town post offices and public buildings. When faced by such local antagonism, many artists changed their original designs to make them more universally appealing. Hence, although the New Deal agencies were fairly tolerant of diversity in style, in the end there developed a certain degree of uniformity among the murals. The urban murals, on the other hand, particularly those of the more sophisticated New York City area, were more daringly modernistic and even at times abstract. This was not only true of the painting and sculpture installed in

Below: Omaha's transportation imagery was adapted by WPA artists.
Right: Max Baum, *Harpist*, 1938, for WNYC studio, New York.

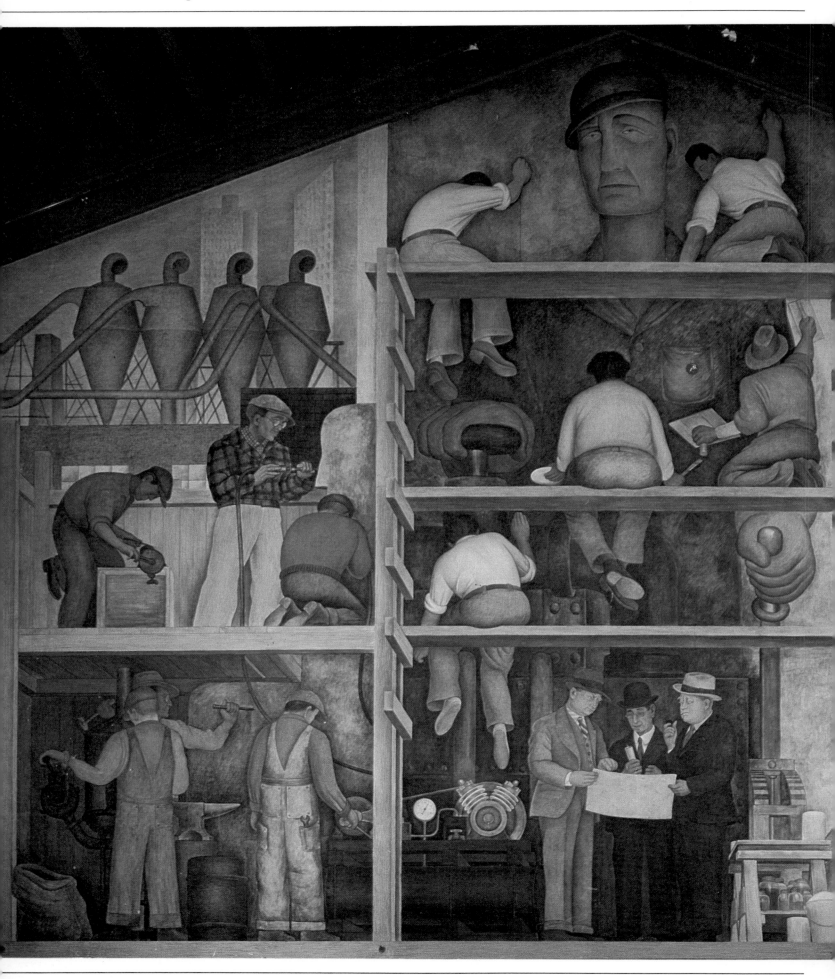

Manhattan's WNYC municipal radio station studios, but also of the art work in schools in New York's outlying boroughs.

Those artists producing smaller paintings under the auspices of the easel project were relatively removed from public scrutiny and therefore enjoyed greater artistic freedom in style and content. The over 100,000 such works produced even included a few art deco paintings, although the bulk represented the genres of American scene regionalism, social realism, and even some abstraction. These paintings ostensibly were meant to be placed in public buildings, but many were unassigned, remained in warehouses, and eventually were unofficially or officially disposed of. And a number of the participating artists understandably resented such bureaucratic requirements as having to punch in at a time clock, and having to meet production quotas.

Many of the more politically radical New Deal muralists revered, and some had even worked as apprentices to, the Mexican muralists Diego Rivera, José Clemente Orozco and David Alfaro Siquieros, who were also active in the United States during the 1930s. Like the Mexicans, some of the American muralists sought to include socially

Left: Diego Rivera, *Making a Fresco*, 1931, San Francisco Art Inst.
Below: Edward Tereda, *Sports*, 1934, Coit Tower, San Francisco.

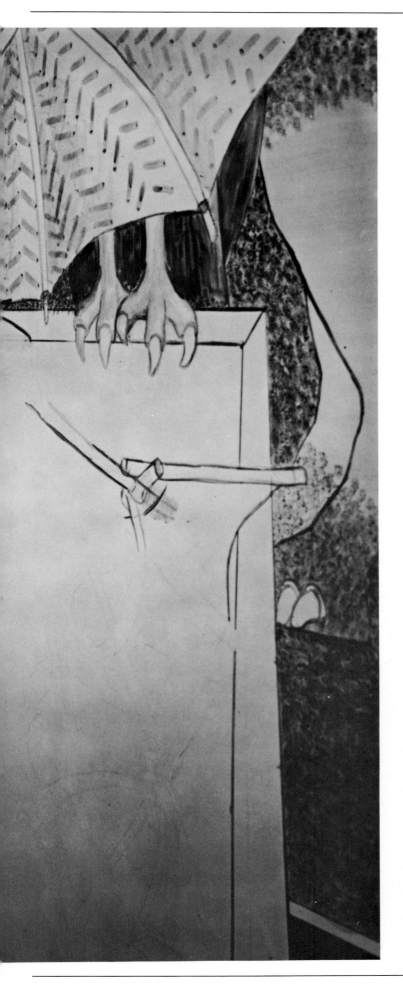

pointed messages in their commissioned works. Such propaganda when discovered, as at San Francisco's Coit Tower, was rarely publicly or officially appreciated and frequently had to be deleted. A cause celebre resulted in 1933 when Diego Rivera's explicitly Marxist and privately commissioned mural was obliterated in Rockefeller Center on the order of John D Rockefeller, Jr. And in 1937 a letter urging Puerto Rican independence had to be painted out on Rockwell Kent's mural, *Delivery of Mail in the Tropics*, in Washington's Post Office Department Building.

Some of the primary beneficiaries of the New Deal art programs were the heretofore socially disadvantaged – particularly blacks and women. Artists from these groups were granted an unprecedented number of important official commissions, as the federal agencies were required to hire such artists in proportions representing their actual numbers in the population as a whole. In addition blacks and women were appointed to a number of key administrative posts in the New Deal art programs. Among the blacks, Sargent Johnson was made a west coast sculpture supervisor and Augusta Savage the director of the Harlem Art Center; and among women, Berenice Abbott headed the WPA photographic division, Elsie Driggs was a New York supervisor, and prominent art deco textile designer Ruth Reeves, who also painted murals, initially directed the Index of American Design.

Mural paintings and architectural sculpture possessing affinities to art deco were produced by several black artists who had risen to prominence during the Harlem Renaissance era. Among the most striking murals were those done by Aaron Douglas for the Countee Cullen branch of the New York Public Library symbolically depicting the cultural and social history of the Afro-Americans. Douglas painted similar works at Fisk Univer-

Left: Rivera and Emmy Lou Packard, mural for Golden Gate Expo.
Below: Harry Gottlieb, *Bootleg Mining*, lithograph, WPA/FAP.

sity, in Chicago, and elsewhere. Other black painters, including Charles Alston in his project for Harlem Hospital, also designed modernist murals influenced by art deco. And sculptor Richmond Barthé, who generally worked in a more realist vein, created elegantly stylized marble relief sculptures — notable was the rhythmically Egyptianate panel entitled *Dance* — for the Harlem River Houses. And in California, San Francisco's Sargent Johnson also produced architectural sculpture and executed a major commission in the form of the Aquatic Park murals for the Golden Gate Exposition.

Generally the artists working on sculptural projects for the New Deal programs had to use, because of budget constraints, such relatively inexpensive and flexible media as cast stone. Cast stone sculptures could not only be carved by hand, but also be reproduced in multiples from the clay or plaster originals once sponsoring institutions could be located. That the art deco influence remained strong in the New Deal sculpture could be seen from Waylande Gregory's elements for a terra cotta fountain group, *Light Dispelling Darkness*, intended for the grounds of Roosevelt Hospital in New Brunswick, New Jersey. The stylized motifs of jagged lightning, clouds, skyscraper, and dirigible here were meant as a symbolic tribute to Thomas Edison, who had invented the electric light not far from the fountain's intended site.

Left: Waylande Gregory, *Light Dispelling Darkness*, circa 1937.
Below: Aaron Goodelman, *Homeless*, circa 1936.

May 17. 1941 **THE** Price 15 cents

NEW YORKER

Above: Virginia Snedeker's cover gently satirized New Deal art.

Apparently there was some degree of tolerance for sculptural works referring to the economic and social miseries of the depression, as seen, for instance, in Aaron Goodelman's *Homeless*, which was conceived in a simplified cubist-influenced style. Probably such statues escaped popular condemnation because they were quite small in size, as opposed to the large-scale figures placed in exterior public locations. Characteristically, many of the more monumental, as well as more modest, freestanding sculptures placed in playgrounds, housing projects, and zoos frequently depicted such politically neutral subject matter as animals, which were frequently stylized in an art deco manner. A superior example of this genre was the sculptural group designed by Edgar Miller for Chicago's Jane Addams Housing Project.

Predictably, a number of the monumental figural statues that were erected did attract their shape of public disapproval. In San Francisco, Beniamino Bufano was able to execute an elegantly stylized red granite and cast aluminum statue of Chinese revolutionary Sun Yat-sen, but his modernist design for a colossal Saint Francis met

with widespread hostility. Peace activist Bufano had achieved notoriety in 1917 by chopping off a finger and mailing it to President Wilson as an antiwar gesture. And in San Diego, Donal Hord's monolithic fountain statue, *Guardian of Water*, raised a public debate over the allegorical figure's resemblance to a Mexican peasant woman. The statue's elegantly decorative mosaic base and the rhythmically patterned stone rim of the fountain basin echoed the luxurious art deco ornament of the 1920s. In California New Deal art, the outdoor mosaic decoration of public buildings experienced a revival, and some of the more important projects were designed and executed by such women artists as Maxine Albro, Marian Simpson, and others.

The most typical New Deal sculptural works were the stylized architectural bas reliefs produced by Chaim Gross, Concetta Scarvaglione, Cesare Stea, and others portraying dignified and heroic laborers involved in agricultural and industrial activities. The classical quality of these compositions was eminently suited to the classical moderne buildings they adorned. Scarvaglione, who later won the coveted Prix de Rome, was an exemplary beneficiary of the wide opportunities opened to women artists. Between 1935 and 1939, she was commissioned to create a number of important relief and freestanding sculptures for the Washington Federal Post Office building, the Federal Trade Commission building, and for the New York World's Fair.

Craftspeople and designers also benefitted from the New Deal programs. A notable project was Timberline Lodge, a United States Forest Service recreational facility built on the slopes of Mount Hood near Portland, Oregon. The rustic 48-bedroom lodge with 10 dormitories and various restaurant and lounge areas was completed under the direction of interior designer Margery Hoffman Smith. Nearly all of the interior fittings and furnishings – including textiles, furniture, carpets, stained glass, mosaics, and metalwork fixtures – were executed by hand by both experienced and inexperienced apprentice artisans in a complex collaborative effort. Subdued art deco influences were visible in the zigzag patterning on some of the curtains and in the design of the upholstered wooden chairs with a low center of gravity. In 1973, Timberline was designated a national historic monument.

New York City's Design Laboratory, co-directed by Gilbert Rohde, offered a professional curriculum in industrial design, textile design, advertising, and photography. Like the Bauhaus, the Design Laboratory tried to apply fine arts principles to industrial production. Policy differences with the school's administration led the WPA to disband it in 1937. Chicago established a similar project, with the assistance of Laszlo Moholy-Nagy, that tackled the design of craft rather than industrial products. And, as noted in the chapter on illustration and graphic art, the New Deal poster project employed commercial artists to produce some 35,000 original designs, the majority of which demonstrated the influence of modernism and had strong affinities to art deco.

Right: Donal Hord with his sculpture *Aztec*. His San Diego fountain statue, *Guardian of Water* provoked a racist controversy.

Above: Timberline Lodge, Mount Hood, near Portland, Oregon, was a New Deal project providing work and training for craftspeople. Mosaics, woodwork **(above right)**, and textile work **(below)** were only some of the many skills developed and practiced there.

These government sponsored visual arts programs allowed the participating artists to develop their talents by working intensively at their craft in a way that would have been difficult during the depression, or even during ordinary times, without such official patronage. The value of the New Deal programs could not be obliterated by the recurring controversies over the quality of the work, its political content, the social purpose of art, and the questionable benefits of democratizing art.

In retrospect, the most disturbing aspect of the New Deal art programs was the wholesale way in which murals and easel paintings were painted over, dismantled, and permanently lost by heedless and hostile caretakers. Such widespread deliberate destruction of art was equaled only by the iconoclastic campaigns that took place in the eighth-century Byzantine Empire and in sixteenth-century Reformation Europe. Only recently has there been a move to reclaim such works as New York City's Bellevue Hospital murals, which include elegant art deco paintings by Emilio Amero, and to restore the vast allegorical mural, *Flight*, by James Brooks in LaGuardia Airport's Marine Air Terminal.

By far the most costly of the New Deal projects were the building programs. After the Wall Street crash of October 1929, there was a time lag before the depression began to affect the construction of new buildings. Those commercial projects already in the process of construction were

Left: James Fraser's *Aspiration and Literature*, Washington, DC.
Below: Michael Lantz, Man Controlling Trade, erected 1942, Washington DC.

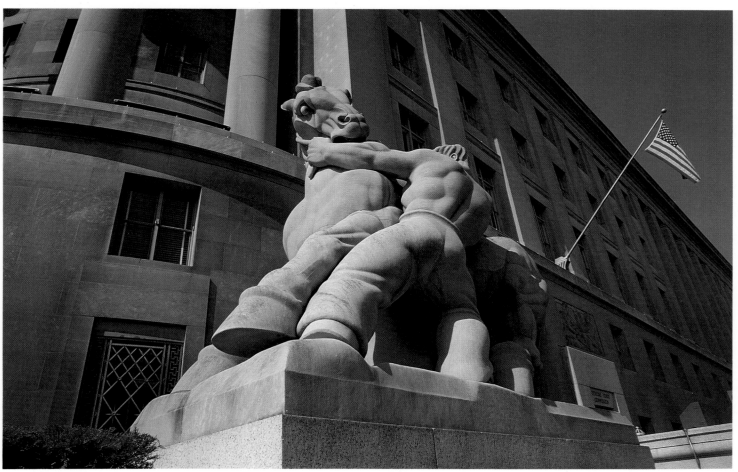

generally completed, although many were to remain at least partially empty for want of tenants. But as unemployment spread in the building trades as well, the Public Works Administration (PWA) was established in 1933 in order to increase employment and to improve the economy through the construction of needed civic buildings and other public works projects. Often the PWA provided only part of the necessary building costs; the rest had to be raised by local taxes.

The architectural style of the PWA buildings was not dictated as a matter of official policy. Rather, frequently the shortages of specific materials and certain restrictions accounted for some degree of uniformity. The classical moderne style already in use, with its massiveness and restrained ornament, was found to be functionally and symbolically ideal for many of the PWA projects, although colonial revival styles were also a popular choice. The plans for the individual buildings originated in or had to be approved in Washington, and the projects were supervised by PWA personnel. The actual construction could be supervised by the architects. The PWA projects basically were designed to put experienced construction workers back on the job.

A second New Deal agency, the Works Progress Administration (WPA) was created in 1935, and it also became involved with federally sponsored construction projects, using them to employ skilled workers, as well as a means to train unskilled workers for new trades. Therefore, while PWA projects operated on a fairly high level of professionalism — with skilled laborers, competitive bidding for contractors, and on site supervision by architects — WPA projects were far more frustrating for the architects. WPA projects required that most of the budget be spent on labor and that work be completed within one year. Hence, unskilled workers were placed in positions to receive on the job training, they were overseen by teaching supervisors instead of by the architect, and the architect had to act as his own general contractor. Many of the WPA projects involved renovations or repairs to already existing facilities.

But despite the various built-in inefficiencies of these government programs, particularly of the WPA, there was an undeniable net advantage — by the end of the decade, countless communities nationwide possessed civic facilities they might never have built otherwise and hundreds of architects remained gainfully employed. Thanks to the PWA, many of these buildings, with their restrained art deco modernism, have endured to the present day as dignified and impressive monuments of a unique era in American history.

Below: Fire Department Headquarters, Sparks, Nevada.
Right: Francis Keally, Oregon State Capitol, Salem, 1936-38, north entrance.

8
EXPOSITIONS

From the late 1920s through the 1930s, three major American expositions were planned and erected. These were the 1933 Chicago Century of Progress Exposition, the 1939 San Francisco Golden Gate Exposition, and the 1939-1940 New York World's Fair which had as its theme the World of Tomorrow. Almost all of the era's major architects, artists and designers — many of whom were prominent producers of art deco works – were involved to a greater or lesser degree in the planning of and the execution of ideas for these extravaganzas. In addition, smaller exhibitions organized within the context of the larger expositions brought together the latest decorative arts, photography, painting, and sculpture, much of which also had close affinities to art deco. And furthermore, the expositions disseminated posters, diverse written and pictorial materials, and other souvenirs that required the services of graphic artists and others to create designs that aptly reflected the style and content of each particular exposition. Thus, these expositions not only summed up the important artistic trends of the time, but they also expressed in subtle and overt ways the concerns and aspirations of American society as a whole.

During the decades between the wars, more modest exhibitions had also played an essential role in informing the American public of and gaining acceptance for modernist furniture, household accessories, and other artifacts in the art deco style. These exhibitions, arranged first by department stores and later by galleries and museums, featured the work of the finest European designers, advanced developments in American furniture and interior design, and fostered collaboration between designers and industry. But despite the public nature of these exhibitions, they reached only a relatively small and élite audience of educated consumers located in New York and other major cities, as well as interested modernist architects and designers and progressive industrialists. Most of these exhibitions were also reported and frequently illustrated in museum publications and special-

ized periodicals, thus reaching others who were also interested but unable to attend.

The world's fairs, on the other hand, were conceived for a mass audience and generally tended to sum up recent architectural design, and other artistic trends rather than introduce new ideas in these areas. The department store and museum exhibitions, however, were able to present design movements while they were still evolving. Nevertheless, the world's fairs had a powerful impact in other areas — in the realm of technological innovation, and of sophisticated psychological conditioning of consumers. Hence the fairs were accused by some critics of promoting commercialism while remaining artistically conservative.

This kind of ambivalent influence was one that also characterized the two most important American expositions preceding those of the 1930s. These were the 1876 Philadelphia Centennial Exposition and the 1893 World Columbian Exposition in Chicago. The 1876 Philadelphia exposition was organized to celebrate the 100 years anniversary of the nation's independence. Following not so long after the political uncertainties raised by the Civil War, the 1876 exposition attempted to reiterate the essential democratic principles on which the United States had been founded. The Philadelphia exposition highlighted as well a period of remarkable industrial growth. Foreign visitors to the exposition were greatly impressed by the exhibits demonstrating such American technological advances as innovations in machinery and tools, but they were openly contemptuous of the displays of American furniture, which they criticized as poorly made and lacking in "magnificence." Therefore, although the exposition appropriately celebrated the nation's political foundations and industrial skill, it also pointed out glaring inadequacies in American design and the arts. But in the following decades, this public acknowledgment of American shortcomings in artistic endeavors served as a very effective impetus to the development of the subsequent Arts and Crafts Movement, which placed a high value on good design and excellent workmanship.

The 1893 World Columbian Exposition in Chicago marked the first time in the United States that a group of

Left: Raymond Hood, Apartment House Loggia for 1929 exhibit, *The Architect and the Industrial Arts*, Metropolitan Museum of Art.

leading architects, painters, and sculptors had been called together to collaborate on such an event. The topographical plan for the exposition was developed by prominent landscape architect Frederick Law Olmstead, who converted a marshy wasteland into an arcadian setting of islands, ponds and lagoons. The majority of the fair structures were designed in an impressively ornate, but retrograde classicistic Beaux Arts style based on renaissance and baroque prototypes. The outstanding exception was Louis Sullivan's orientalist Transportation Building. Among the important architects who worked on the 'White City,' as the fair became popularly known, were McKim, Mead and White; Peabody and Stearns; and Van Brunt and Howe. Although their classically-influenced buildings were seen as an appropriate way to express the nation's emergence as an imperial power, they set back the development of modern architecture, according to Sullivan, by some 50 years. A number of large American cities rushed to plan similarly grandiose civic complexes, and classical revival styles became the choice of many influential builders. Social critics of the Columbian exposition cited the inappropriateness of such a "city beautiful" — so gleamingly clean, rationally ordered, and isolated both physically and ideologically from the widespread urban slums that blighted an era marked by economic depression, rampant unemployment, and struggles by the rising labor movement to lessen the omnipotence of the industrialists. Four decades later, similar charges justifiably could be levelled by social

critics against the expositions of the 1930s. Those fairs also could be regarded as escapist fantasies that failed to confront the issues of the nation's severest economic crisis yet.

Chicago's second world's fair, the 1933 Century of Progress Exposition, may not have been accused of artistic conservatism at the time, but nevertheless it was predictably marked by controversy in planning and execution. Intended to commemorate 100 years of Chicago's existence as a city, the fair was also an opportunity to demonstrate the lessons American architects and designers had learned from the 1925 Paris decorative arts exposition. The Chicago Century of Progress Exposition was first proposed in 1927, during the height of American prosperity. The fair's board of directors asked architect Raymond Hood to organize a design board to plan the expostion layout and structures. Hood, himself the designer of a number of monuments of art deco architecture, invited others active in art deco design to join his committee. Among these architects and designers were Harvey Wiley Corbett, Paul Philippe Cret, John Wellborn Root, Hubert Burnham and Ralph T Walker.

The fact that Frank Lloyd Wright was not included among the fair's architects resulted in some speculation. Wright had left Chicago in 1916 for Japan and California. According to some reports Wright, despite his financial difficulties resulting from the depression, rejected several proposals that he design fair buildings after he had been informed that he would not be permitted to design the entire project. Another report described a 1931 Town Hall meeting called to protest Wright's exclusion. At this

Below: An unrealized proposal for the 1933 Chicago exposition.

164

gathering, Wright submitted several visionary proposals for the fair, including a colossal woven steel canopy to cover the entire fair, the inclusion of floating elements, and a half-mile high skyscraper. Also, there were probably justifiable fears among the other architects that if Wright participated, he would not cooperate with his fellow builders. In any case, America's most innovative architect was not represented at the 1933 Chicago fair.

At the end of 1928, preliminary proposals were submitted by the design committee members. Among the suggested fair features were a system of moving sidewalks and escalators conveying visitors to entrances located on the tops of terraced multistory buildings; a network of canals for silent electric motorboats; a dynamic nighttime lighting display resembling a 'giant piece of jewelry'; and a lagoon-based aluminum tower acting as a volcano of light and water. The intervening great depression led to the necessary abandonment of most of the more experimental and costly proposals. Norman Bel Geddes, who was hired by the design committee as a consultant in 1929, also had several proposals rejected – including one for a dance restaurant built on four islands, interconnected by bridges and illuminated by neon tube arches ('the largest beacon in the world'); and another for an underwater aquarium restaurant. For the layout of the exposition, various symmetrical site plans (hitherto used for previous

Right: Norman Bel Geddes, model of revolving aerial restaurant for Chicago fair. The depression made such projects impractical.
Below: Structure housing the exhibit showing the generation, distribution, and utilization of electricity. Chicago, 1933.

Above: General Electric 'House of Magic' exhibit, Chicago, 1933.
Above right: Albert Kahn's General Motors Building, Chicago, 1933.
Below right: Travel & Transport Building, **left,** Chicago, 1933.

world's fairs) were considered but rejected, and an asymmetrical plan – 'the unplanned planning solution' – was eventually employed. In 1932, Joseph Urban was appointed director of color for the fair, with Lee Lawrie as sculptural consultant and Walter D'Arcy Ryan as director of illumination.

In the end, the design commission achieved its goal for creating an exposition 'radically different' from earlier world's fairs. The buildings erected specifically for the exposition incorporated a variety of art deco motifs, including skyscraper style setbacks, cubist-influenced volumes and cylindrical shapes, decorative geometric surface patterning, stylized relief sculpture, innovative use of glass and other machine age materials, and modernist interiors. The diversity of architectural forms was unified by the use of brilliant coloristic effects. Under Urban's direction, a range of 23 vivid hues was employed to create a 'natural sequence' between the buildings. Most buildings bore three or four colors each. At night an elaborate choreography of floodlights and neon transformed the fair into a magical spectacle. Enthusiastic commentators nicknamed the exposition the 'Rainbow City,' which at night metamorphosed into a 'paint factory on fire.'

Among the fair's notable architectural designs were Cret's Hall of Science; Albert Kahn's General Motors building, which contained a complete automobile assembly plant; Holabird and Root's Chrysler building; Nicolai and Faro's *Time, Fortune* and *Architectural Forum* building surmounted with colossal photomurals; Kahn's cylindrical Ford Motor building symbolically designed to represent an automobile gear; and George Fred Keck's 12-sided House of Tomorrow. The Travel and Transport Building, designed by E H Bennett, Hubert Burnham and J A Holabird, mounted a green body on a yellow base and steel trusses painted blue supported the building's suspended dome by means of cables linked to 12 towers, in much the same way as suspension bridges were erected. The walls themselves were of sheet metal, bolted and clipped together. The Travel and Transport Building's central window was enlivened by the characteristic art deco rising sun motif, with a band of geometric patterning at the top. As may be seen from the construction of this building, the innovative

Above: Raymond Hood, Electric Building and Communications Building with electric cascades and gilded pylons, Chicago, 1933.

use of new materials was an important consideration in the architectural designs for the fair. In addition to sheet metal, other buildings used such materials as prestressed concrete and asbestos board for their walls. Thus, the economic constraints imposed by the depression led to the innovative use of new materials, which in turn lowered the costs of construction.

Elroy Ruiz's Owens-Illinois Glass Company building with its setback skyscraper style central tower, was appropriately constructed of multicolored glass blocks. And among Raymond Hood's designs was the Electric Building, with a curved great court that resembled a dam with water flowing over it – an effect enhanced by the use of blue neon light. The 'dam' was flanked by sculptural relief panels of enormous stylized art deco figures representing atomic energy and stellar energy. On the lagoon side of the court, a pylon gateway was decorated with Aztec-style geometric patterns and sculptural relief figures representing light and sound. As may be surmised from the construction and decoration of the specific buildings, the participating companies frequently used the architecture as a symbolic and often not very subtle way of promoting their own products and services to potential consumers among the fair-going audience.

While this propagandistic use of art and architecture predictably led critics to decry the commercialism of the fair, this was on the other hand only the continuation of a longstanding artistic tradition. For millenia, pharaohs, emperors, and church authorities had used painting, sculpture, and architecture to promote political and religious ideas. What was new here was the promotion of economic and technological ideas. The same could also be said of much of the spectacular architecture, architectural ornament, and design in the luxuriant zigzag style art deco of the twenties. The aesthetic ideal of "art for art's sake" was a relatively recent one, allied to the Romantic movement in art and literature.

At the time, the design of the Chicago fair buildings was regarded as self consciously modernistic. Only in retrospect did it become apparent that the exposition's architecture looked fundamentally toward the past. It was closely tied to the polychromatic zigzag deco style of the twenties, while the streamlined style had now become the trend of the future. Indeed, the streamlined style was introduced to the public at the Chicago fair, not in its architectural manifestation, but in its original form – in aerodynamic transportation vehicles dreamed up by the influential participants in the emerging industrial design movement.

The experimental version of E G Budd Company's Burlington Zephyr – a high-speed, diesel-powered train of

lightweight stainless steel construction, designed to go up to 100 miles per hour – made its debut in the second season of the Century of Progress fair. The firm of Paul Philippe Cret had been responsible for the design and ornamentation of the train interior in art deco style. Cret's other and later interior work for the Budd Company included an elaborate 1920s style design of stylized animal and floral imagery for the California Zephyr. Apparently commercial clients saw a zigzag interior as compatible with a streamlined exterior. At any rate, public interest in the Zephyr was enormous, as some 709,000 exposition visitors stood in line to tour the train. Another high point of the fair was the introduction of Buckminster Fuller's teardrop shaped, airflow, three-wheeled Dymaxion car (the name was derived from the words, 'dynamism,' 'maximum,' and 'ions'), which appeared in 'Wings of a Century,' a pageant recounting the history of transportation.

The fair received mixed reviews. Many of those architects who did not participate were severely critical. Frank Lloyd Wright found it 'pretty, strident and base,' terming it 'wholesale imitation, hit or miss, of the genuine forms that occurred in out-of-the-way places many years ago.' Ralph Adams Cram saw the fair as incorrigibly ugly, 'a casual association of the gasometer, the freight-yard and the grain elevator.' Other more charitable commentators saw the vividly-hued, bustling exposition as optimistically

Left: When light beams from the star Arcturus, traveling since 1893, were picked up by photoelectric tubes at four astronomical observatories, signals flashed on this display board at the Hall of Science to officially light up the 1933 Chicago fair.
Below: The Burlington Zephyr, the first America diesel-powered streamlined passenger train, made its debut at the Chicago fair.

symbolizing a way out of the depression. Regardless of the aesthetic judgments on the fair's architecture, the Chicago exposition did offer a valuable opportunity to test radical new engineering and industrial building methods, as well as to experiment with innovative materials in construction. Thus, in a relatively short period, major advances in building technique were made that ordinarily could have taken decades to evolve on their own. In addition, the fair inaugurated and creatively investigated the possibilities of employing neon lighting as an illumination medium.

Heartening, too, was the public response. By the time the Chicago Century of Progress Exposition closed its gates for the last time in October 1934, over 38 million people had visited the fair. And when the accounts were totalled, it also turned out that the fair had been an outstanding financial success — possibility the first and last such success in the history of American expositions.

The two expositions, in San Francisco and New York, that took place at the end of the decade were quite different from one another in intent and outward appearance, although both granted a prominent place to art deco architecture, sculpture, and related design. Located on man-made Treasure Island in the middle of San Francisco Bay, the 1939 Golden Gate International Exposition was less than half the size of the concurrent New York World's Fair. And while the New York theme of 'World of Tomorrow' was primarily expressed through futuristic-looking streamlined buildings, the San Francisco fair's exotic fantasy architecture focused on the cultures of the Pacific Ocean, for which San Francisco was the major American embarkation port and air terminal. The California fair was also, in part, a celebration of the 1937 completion of the 4200-foot long Golden Gate Bridge, which surpassed by 700 feet New York City's 1931 George Washington Bridge to capture first place as the world's longest suspension bridge.

The architecture of the San Francisco fair was more closely allied to the tradition of ephemeral exposition architecture, which in earlier fairs usually sought to re-create past utopias. The Golden Gate Exposition evoked some lost pre-Columbian paradise, or Oceanic Shangri-la. This dream-like effect was achieved through the combination of stylized, primitivistic sculptures of monolithic figures — such as Ralph Stackpole's 80-foot tall theme statue of 'Pacifica' — with architecture allusive of the Aztec style, an art deco variation popular in California for the past two decades. Characteristic of these exposition structures were Blakewell and Weihe's Elephant Towers, with sculpture by Donald Macky. These stepped zigurrat-shaped towers were reminiscent of the skyscraper style setbacks of the late 1920s, and were suggestive as well of some Southeast Asian temple.

Streamlined art deco made a relatively unobtrusive appearance in the commercial exhibits which generally were grouped together in larger commonly shared structures, instead of occupying individual pavilions as they did at the New York fair. Among these exhibits were the United States Steel Corporation display designed by

Left: Tower of the Sun, Golden Gate Exposition, San Francisco, 1939.

Above: Blakewell & Weihe's Elephant Towers, Golden Gate Exposition. Their Aztec-style setbacks recalled the skyscraper style.

Walter Dorwin Teague, and the Dow Chemical Company exhibit designed by Alden Dow, which made extensive use of glass block construction combined with dramatic illumination by artificial light. And the influence of the true architecture of the future – the austere and ideologically functional International Style – was present in Timothy Pflueger's Federal complex of box-shaped, glass-walled buildings.

There was also another side to the criticism that the San Francisco and other expositions of the 1930s were escapist fantasies that insensitively ignored the dire social realities of the depression. Escapist indeed they were, and as such they played an essential role in raising the national morale and offering hope for the future. Just as Hollywood producers turned out numerous screwball comedies and Busby Berkeley's upbeat dance extravaganzas during the depression years as a vital antidote to the pervasive gloom, so did the expositions help to relieve what also could have become an incurable national psychological depression. President Franklin D Roosevelt, of course, had recognized this basic fact of human nature with his inaugural challenge of 'the only thing we have to fear is fear itself' – thus tacitly admitting that the perception of a reality was just as important, if not more so, than the reality itself. Therefore, if people could be reassured of the enduring positive aspects and optimistic possibilities of life, they could then nurture the spiritual determination necessary to persevere and eventually to overcome such temporal, though devastating, difficulties as the great depression.

The 1939 New York World's Fair, which apotheosized the streamlined phase of art deco architectural design,

was far more ambitious in physical expanse and thematic intent than the Golden Gate Exposition. Originally proposed in 1935 by a group of New York businessmen, the fair was envisioned as a mechanism by which to revitalize the economically stressed New York metropolitan area. These aspirations were based to no small extent on the profit reaped by the recently ended Chicago Century of Progress Exposition. Ostensibly, the aim of the fair was to celebrate the 150th anniversary of George Washington's inauguration as the nation's first president in New York City's Federal Hall.

But the ensuing debate over the theme and content of the proposed fair was won by a functionalist faction which included Lewis Mumford, Harvey Wiley Corbett, Gilbert Rohde, and Walter Dorwin Teague. This group's detailed plan for the 'World of Tomorrow' outlined the presentation of exhibits exploring the possibilities of a planned social environment – an ideal industrial planning solution facilitated by the essential role of the machine. This futuristic utopia was to be visually expressed by means of streamlined style architecture and design.

Among the planners and executors of the 'World of Tomorrow' were the nation's leading architects and industrial designers. Besides Teague and Rohde, the participants included Norman Bel Geddes, Henry Dreyfuss, Raymond Loewy, Egmont Arens, George Sakier, Donald Deskey, Russel Wright, Edward Durrell Stone, Morris Lapidus, Albert Kahn, Alvar Aalto, and Ely Jacques Kahn. Hugh Ferriss, highly regarded for his romantic renderings of 1920s style art deco skyscrapers, was

Below: Augusta Savage, *The Harp ('Lift Every Voice and Sing')*, 1939.

appointed the fair's official architectural delineator. Graphic designer Joseph Binder was invited to create a prize-winning poster design which became the basis for the most widely displayed poster in modern times. And the roster of participating painters and sculptors was a most impressive one – included were Alexander Calder, Waylande Gregory, Isamu Noguchi, Hildreth Meiere, Paul Manship, Rockwell Kent, Fernand Leger, Lyonel Feininger, Salvador Dali, Ruth Reeves, Augusta Savage, Concetta Scarvaglione, William Zorach, Ilya Bolotowsky, Arshile Gorky, Philip Guston, Willem de Kooning, Carl Milles and Stuart Davis.

With a few exceptions, the exposition's murals and sculpture fell within art deco's canon of decorative or heroic figural stylization, and many of the artworks were symbolically or allegorically related to their particular building's function or sponsor. The most advanced – that is, abstract – murals were done under the auspices of the Works Progress Administration Federal Arts Project. There was on the part of the more innovative WPA artists a self-conscious sense of competition with the more artistically conservative but also commercially more successful artists still working in the art deco style.

The exposition's sculpture was apparently an afterthought and its range was broad, although the majority of works were monumental stylized and frequently allegorical figural groups. Typically, the more conservative works were those officially commissioned by the Fair Commission. *The Harp ('Lift Every Voice and Sing')* was representative of this tendency, although it was atypical in that its creator, Augusta Savage, was the only black artist to receive a fair commission. On the other hand, private industry tended to commission more experimental works. For example, Albert Kahn and Walter Dorwin Teague, the architect and the designer of the Ford Motor Company's streamlined pavilion, selected Isamu Noguchi to create a constructivist *Chassis Fountain*, and Robert Foster to design a stainless steel sculpture of the god *Mercury* (also the name of one of Ford's car models) to go above the building's main entrance. The stylized *Mercury* was still recognizably art deco, but in its use of industrial materials and welded openwork construction, it already pointed toward post World War II trends. Foster also made an even more abstract sculpture of welded steel, called *Textiles*, for the fair. And from Consolidated Edison, Alexander Calder received an unusual commission to design a fountain and to choreograph for it a water, color, and light performance by synchronized jets of water.

But by far the most imposing sculptures of the fair were the stark white 610-foot tall Trylon (triangular pylon) and the 180-foot wide globe known as the Perisphere, along with its 950-foot long spiral ramp, or Helicline. The symbol of the fair, this monumental cubist grouping designed by Wallace Harrison and J. André Fouilhoux, was not just sculpture but also architecture. Visitors rode what was then the world's longest escalator part way up the Trylon and then entered the Perisphere where they

Above: A model-sized version of the Trylon and Perisphere.
Right: Henry Dreyfuss' Democracity diorama inside the Perisphere.

173

viewed Democracity, an enormous multimedia diorama of a futuristic urban and exurban complex. At night, the exterior of the Perisphere served as a colossal screen for multiple projections of changing colors and of moving clouds, as well as representational images tied to special events such as Thomas Edison's birthday.

The most impressive element of the fair was its architecture, which evoked a science fiction film set. This effect was achieved by the multiplicity of sculptural streamlined pavilions – particularly dramatic were those commissioned by such industrial sponsors as General Motors, Ford Motor Company, the Radio Corporation of America, Chrysler and others. The predominantly art deco styling also carried over to the smaller commercial pavilions, many of which were emblematic of their product. The Schaefer Center, for example, sported the popular horizontal streamlined style striping and was topped by a tower in the shape of a stylized frozen fountain. This had been an important art deco motif in the 1920s style, but in the exposition context it referred to the beverages produced by Schaefer.

In general, contemporary architectural critics found little to admire in the futuristic exposition architecture. They condemned its crass commercialism, its hybrid nature, its superficial 'modernity,' and its 'decorative touches.' The foreign pavilions, however, which were mostly executed in the austere International Style, received their wholehearted approval. This attitude was to become the status quo for the academic and critical architectural establishment over the next several decades as, beginning with the 1932 Museum of Modern Art's International Style exhibition, proponents of this style were able to suppress to a remarkable degree most divergent and pluralistic tendencies in modern architectural design. It is only in recent years, therefore, that the exposition architecture – and art deco architecture in general – became a subject of professional appreciation and that serious study focused on its complex symbolic implications and on its reflection of the historical milieu and cultural values of the decades between the wars.

But despite such negative critical judgments at the time of the New York World's Fair and its structures, the visitors to the exposition were overwhelmingly enthusiastic. The World of Tomorrow theme provided a welcome fantasy at the end of a grim decade, and the technological marvels and the new consumer products on display – including robots, a synthetic speech synthesizer, the superhighways of the Futurama exhibit, television, and labor-saving household appliances – appeared accessible to most and indeed did seem to promise a brighter future.

Much thought by the participating industrial designers had gone into planning the logical sequence and organization of the buildings, effective pedestrian traffic flows, and psychologically compelling multimedia display techniques to promote the utopian ideals, the technological advances and the new consumer products that were the

Left: The Trylon and Perisphere under construction.
Right: The Trylon and Perisphere were the World of Tomorrow's unifying symbol, New York World's Fair, 1939.

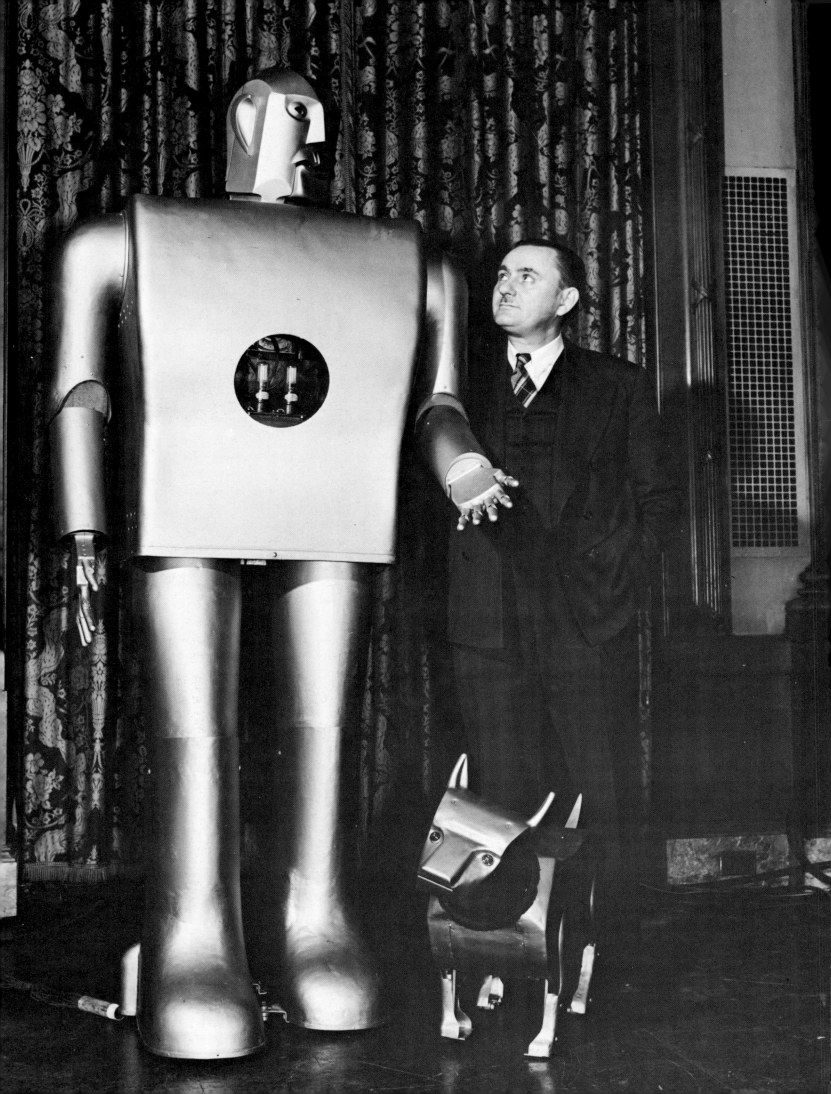

core of the exposition. But not all exhibiting companies shared their futuristic mind set. Of the 15 model homes on display in the 'Town of Tomorrow,' fully two-thirds were traditional, with Colonial Revival as the favored style.

The new ideas in architecture and design introduced by the World of Tomorrow fair were actually quite limited in scope. As most of the temporary futuristic buildings were made of customary exposition plaster and stucco, there was little opportunity to investigate new materials and building techniques. What imaginative design solutions there were had been applied to the exposition's accessory structures, such as the Aqualon fountains which resembled outsized radio vacuum tubes filled with swimming goldfish. Again, one of the most exciting aspects of the New York fair was the lighting design, this time featuring fluorescent tubing in all kinds of innovative machine aesthetic lighting fixtures and incorporated as well into the exterior building walls to create decorative and striking nighttime effects. Architecturally, therefore, the New York World's Fair did not so much predict the future, as sum up the past decade. In effect, the exposition was the grand finale of the streamlined art deco style.

But the New York fair also reflected wider cultural and international political concerns of the 1930s. The preoccupation of the fair's planners with behavioral control and psychological conditioning techniques underlined certain features that the fair, and the art deco style as a whole, had in common with the art, architecture, social goals, and propaganda of the totalitarian governments of Nazi Germany, fascist Italy, and Soviet Russia.

Perhaps emblematic of the connections between art deco and fascism were the robots that were such a popular feature of the New York fair. As machines in human form they echoed the persistent machine aesthetic trend in art deco sculpture – that of idealizing the human figure until it shed all individuality and finally came to resemble a gleaming and perfect machine. With their low tolerance for individualism the fascists also preferred, in art and life, idealized people in the heroic mode, repetitive cogs in a vast social machine, who functioned in perfect synchrony. Similarly, the fascist predilection for mass athletic displays of calisthenics conducted in mechanical unison had an American counterpart in the synchronized dance choreography of Busby Berkeley. Notable too was the fascist taste for monumental classicized architecture, a style that was also favored by the New Deal building programs which were instrumental in spreading classical moderne architecture across the continent. But in the end, the intent of art deco, though also utopian in its streamlined style, but it also provided a final public forum political motives of the fascists.

The New York World's Fair not only summed up the streamlined style, but it also provided a final public forum for the imagery and themes of art deco as a whole. And all this was the product of architects, designers, and artists working in collaboration, as they had done so on so many

Above: Glass brick facade of Metals Building, with a light standard to the left, New York World's Fair, 1939.

earlier art deco projects. Here once more the artists and designers visualized, in sculptures and murals, America's love affair with the technological marvels of the modern age – transportation and communications – as seen in the stylized representations of airplanes, locomotives, ocean liners, automobiles, bridges, radios, electrical power networks, and industrial production facilities. Present too were those mythologized images of man confidently occupying his niche in the cosmos and, more mundanely, in the workplace. This was quite possibly the last time that man would be shown as so at home in the technological age and so sure of his place in the universe.

Left: Electro the Moto-Man and his dog Sparko, with their creator J M Barnett, a Westinghouse engineer. New York World's Fair, 1939.
Right: Model of Albert Kahn's General Motors complex, housing Norman Geddes' Highways and Horizons exhibit, New York, 1939.

9 REVIVAL

During the late 1960s, collectors, art historians and designers began to focus new attention on the art deco artifacts, furniture, ornamental motifs, and architecture of the 1920s and 1930s. This fresh appreciation originated with the important 1966 Paris exhibition at the Musée des Arts Décoratifs, *Les Années 25, Art Deco/Bauhaus/Stijl/ Esprit Nouveau.* Considered thus on an equal footing with other long-esteemed design movements of the early twentieth century, art deco gained a new respectability. Several influential books followed, the most important of these for the American audience being Bevis Hillier's 1968 *Art Deco of the Twenties and Thirties.*

And American museums, too, began to direct their efforts toward rehabilitating art deco. In 1970, the Finch College Museum of Art held an art deco exhibition that received wide coverage in the New York press. In the following year, the Minneapolis Institute of Arts organized a more extensive historical survey, again with a greater emphasis on European design. The text for the comprehensive catalog, *The World of Art Deco* – later issued as a book – was written, once more, by Hillier.

As interest in specifically American art deco design increased, the Finch College Museum presented a 1973 exhibition on American art deco architecture. By this time, interest was widespread, and exhibitions in other parts of the United States followed. Notable among these was the 1976 show at Syracuse University, *The Art Deco Environment,* which included many hitherto under-valued art deco American ceramics from the museum's own collections. Articles on art deco appeared in a number of specialized and popular periodicals. These were followed by a variety of books on particular aspects of American art deco design – considered were the sky-scraper style in New York City, Rockefeller Center and other key buildings, individual designers – including those of the industrial design movement, and the stream-lined phased of art deco. Research on American modern-istic designers and their creations continued into the 1980s, and resulted in two landmark 1984 exhibits, accompanied by scholarly books. These were the Detroit Institute of Art's *The Cranbrook Vision: Design in America* and Yale University Art Gallery's *Manhattan Between the Wars.*

In 1966, yet another book was published that did not explicitly discuss the art deco style but nevertheless was influential in eventually earning acceptance for American

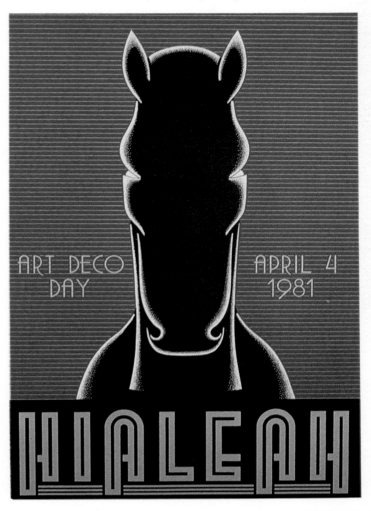

Left: Paul Schulze, *New York, New York,* 1984, Steuben Glass.
Right: Hialeah poster, 1981, designed by Woody Vondracek.

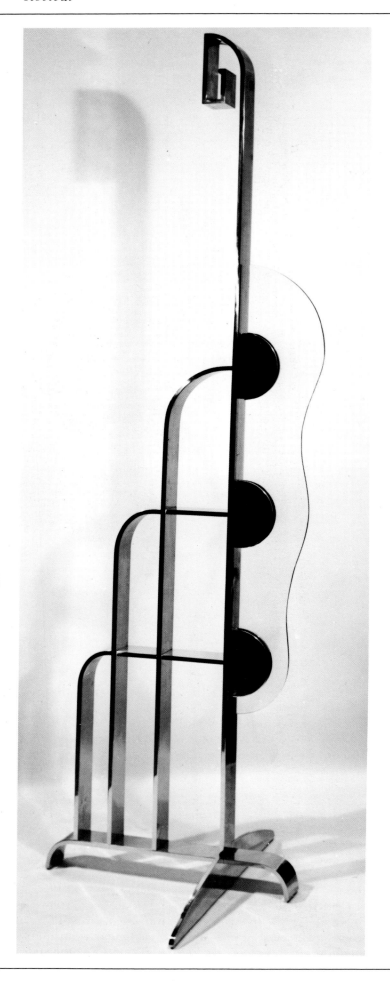

art deco architecture by the academic and professional architectural establishment. This was architect Robert Venturi's *Complexity and Contradiction in Architecture*, a book which created a theoretical justification for the adaption of various historical and vernacular styles and ornament in the contemporary design context. At the time, this was a revolutionary assault on the views long held and promulgated by the theorists and practitioners of the then preeminent International Style who rejected absolutely the use of any ornament, historically based or otherwise. Implicit in Venturi's discussion was a renewed attention to the cultural and symbolic meanings of architecture. Thus, as a style that placed a high value on historically derived and eclectic ornament, and on the symbolic meaning of the building and its decoration, art deco was accorded a new validity.

In the United States, the revived appreciation of art deco architecture was more than purely aesthetic. It also had a much more urgent pragmatic end. A number of the nation's important art deco buildings had already been demolished – among them were such treasures as Joseph Urban's Ziegfeld Theater in New York City, Cincinnati's Union Terminal, and the Atlantic Richfield Building in Los Angeles. And countless other monuments were in similar danger. The widespread recognition of art deco as a valid, complex, and unique historical style helped to focus efforts on gaining for threatened buildings historical landmark status so that they could be saved and preserved. A notable early success in this strategy was Timothy Pflueger's splendid Oakland Paramount Theater, which was entered into the National Registry of Historic Places in 1973 after it had been purchased by the Oakland Symphony and authentically renovated. In 1977, the theater, considered second only in magnificence to New York's Radio City Music Hall, was declared a national landmark.

Another major success of the preservationists came in 1979, when one square mile of Old Miami Beach was officially declared a historic district by the National Registry of Historic Places. The site of some 400 buildings, most of them in the tropical deco style, Old Miami Beach was the first such district with structures erected less than 50 years ago. But despite such fruitful efforts, other significant art deco monuments, such as New York City's Women's House of Detention, were felled by the wrecker's ball.

The renewed appreciation of the historical art deco style also fueled a revival of the style that began in the late 1960s. Early among those producing works that displayed an affinity for, or incorporated art deco motifs were two artists in the vanguard of the New York art world. During the late 1960s, Frank Stella produced a series of decorative geometric paintings composed of precisely segmented arcs or rays of vivid color. This 1968 *Variations on a Circle Series* was strikingly reminiscent of the stylized geometric patterns of art deco. At about the same time, Pop artist Roy Lichtenstein deliberately included in a nostalgic way art deco motifs in paintings, graphic works, and even in sculpture.

Left: Roy Lichtenstein, *Modern Sculpture with Glass Wave,* 1967.

Above: Miriam Wosk, illustrations for Georges Kaplan ads.

Commercial artists were quick to exploit art deco motifs for their novelty, thus creating a new trend in the graphic arts. Of particular interest for these artists were art deco's vividly colored abstract geometric patterns. These were adapted and redesigned by such prominent designers as Milton Glaser and Norman Green for use in posters, book covers, record album covers, new art deco typefaces, and environmental graphics. Art deco imagery also became popular in fashion advertisements and commercial illustration. Some designers 'borrowed' geometric borders directly from the interiors of landmark art deco buildings. Other users of the style – foremost among whom was Milton Glaser's and Seymour Chwast's Push Pin Studios – worked more innovatively, creating paraphrases that were often used in a playful spirit in the contemporary context of the 1970s.

And after the initial art deco revival abated, the style remained in the commercial art vocabulary. In a selection of the best graphic designs of 1983, for example, art deco continued as a strong contender among the various design options. But now there was less interest in its geometric patterns and more in adaptations of specific nostalgic imagery – including looming ocean liners like those by Cassandre, dramatically silhouetted skyscraper skylines, speeding streamlined locomotives, and elegantly stylized human and animal figures. And advertising illustrations designed for stores alluded to a more glamorous era by including stylized palm trees, flamingos, DC-8 propeller airplanes, and skyscraper skylines, sometimes all at one time.

Craftspeople also saw art deco as an inspiration for lively and attractive contemporary designs. Such textile works as pieced quilts were a particularly amenable medium for the geometric and cubist motifs of the style.

1910 White Chair, his 1929 Blue Chair, and his elaborately veneered and inlaid armchair and round table designed in 1929-1930 for his Cranbrook residence. Related furniture, similarly reissued, included Josef Hoffmann's 1913 Via Gallia armchair and sofa, and various tables, chairs, and stools by Alvar Aalto. Not coincidentally, 1984 was the year of major museum exhibitions on Cranbrook Academy designs, the Vienna Secession and Wiener Werkstätte, and of Aalto's work. And the new respect accorded to historical art deco furniture and accessories was paralleled by ever-rising prices whenever authenticated pieces were auctioned.

The work of a number of fine furniture artisans of the late 1970s and 1980s either was inspired by art deco, or bore close affinities to it. The hand made, one of a kind pieces of Judy Kensley McKie, although not overtly based on art deco motifs, were designed in a spirit similar to that which informed the luxurious French deco style furniture of the twenties. A close study of African primitive art, as well as of pre-Columbian, Eskimo, American Indian, early Egyptian and archaic Greek artifacts provided sources for McKie's elegant stylized animal and floral forms, and repetitive geometric patterning of her *Leopard Couch*, *Fish Chest*, and *Frog Cabinet*.

Similarly to the architects of the 1920s and 1930s, those of contemporary times began to design furniture and other accessories appropriate to their architectural interiors. Two leading American architects openly appreciative of art deco, Robert Venturi and Michael Graves, broadened their design ideas to include furniture in the art deco mode. Both architects designed chairs

Above: Cardozo Hotel poster, designed by Woody Vondracek.
Right: Push Pin Studio, poster for Penny Pitch Game, 1968.

Art deco was also a widely used resource for jewelry designers, and of makers of metalware and household accessories. Ceramicists also adapted art deco's geometric designs and cubist shapes, as well as its stylized floral and figural motifs. A number of craftspeople even gave their works titles that specifically alluded to the historical art deco era.

During its revival, the art deco style also became influential in furniture design, resulting in such mass produced pieces as a white lacquered streamlined bedroom ensemble complete with speed stripes, skyscraper style brass beds, and black lacquered 'post modern' dressing tables, also in the skyscraper style, with reeded stripes achieved by glueing rattan strips to mahogany. Other smaller mass produced accessories included such items as clocks encased in miniature ceramic or metal DC-8 planes, figurines of languorous sylphs, and photograph frames of black glass silkscreened with white 'deco geometrics.'

The mass production of such popular art deco revival furniture designs was followed in the 1980s by the resumption of production of selected original historical art deco furniture. Among the chosen pieces were Eliel Saarinen's

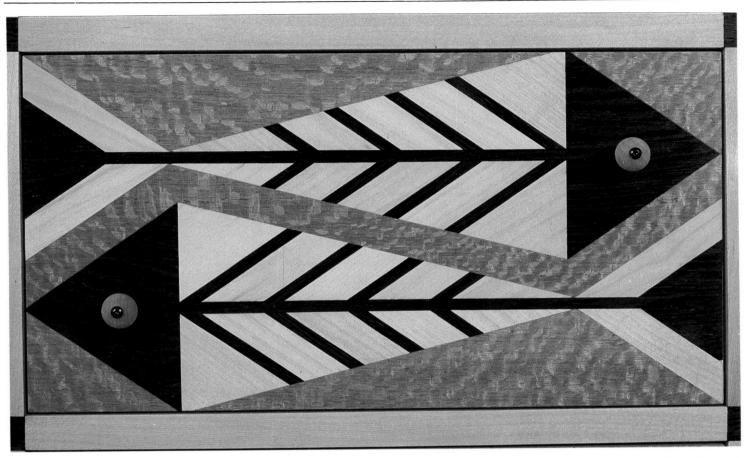

Above: Judy Kensley McKie, *Fish Cabinet* (detail), 1983.

playfully adapting in a caricaturish way art deco features. In his 1984 collection for Knoll International, Venturi created chairs of cut out, laminated molded plywood representing art deco and other historical styles. The art deco influenced furniture of Michael Graves – such as his

Below: Judy Kensley McKie, *Leopard Couch*, 1983.

lounge chair, with its exaggerated shapes and angles and its applied geometric ornament – did not refer to specific historical prototypes; rather it whimsically alluded to art deco as a style. Similarly, in a 1984 line of furniture for Georg Kovacs, graphic designer Seymour Chwast created a series of 'retrograde modern' chairs, some of which in their bold geometric shapes and vivid colors were reminiscent of art deco, even though they were not based on recognizable prototypes.

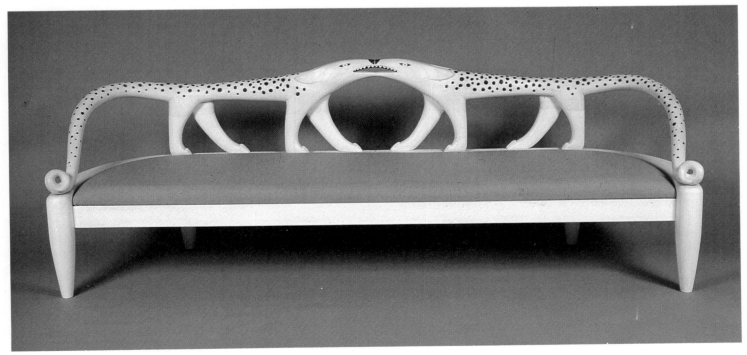

Above: Judy Kensley McKie, *Fish Cabinet*, 1983, lacewood, maple, wenge.

The renewed interest on the part of enlightened manufacturers was demonstrated by a 1984 project sponsored by the Formica Corporation in which 19 furniture designers created impressive handmade furniture. Cabinets, tables, desks, chairs, and screens included references to art deco, as the vividly hued new material was innovatively exploited for its graphic and ornamental effects, and for its ability to accommodate a seamless volumetric appearance.

1984 was also a year in which the design and architectural establishment showed a new interest in other household accessories in the art deco style. Not only did Noritake resume production of Frank Lloyd Wright's

Eliel Saarinen's armchair **(top)**, credenza **(above)**, lounge chair **(top right)**, and dining room side chair **(above right)** – all designed in

1929-30 for his own residence at Cranbrook Academy – were made available to the public in 1984 by Arkitektura.

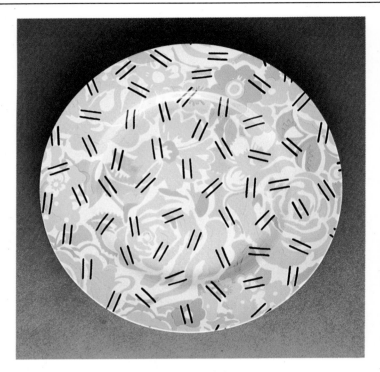

Above: Robert Venturi, 'Grandmother' china, 1984.

Above: Laurinda Spear, 'Miami' china, 1984.

china for the Tokyo Imperial Hotel, but the New York firm of Swid Powell commissioned such leading designer/architects as Venturi, Laurinda Spear, Stanley Tigerman, Robert Stern, Richard Meier and others to design china, crystal, and silver. A number of these items, with their geometric patterning, cubist influenced designs, and vivid colors bore a close affinity to the art deco style. In the previous year, the Italian firm of Alessi introduced limited edition coffee and tea services by 11

leading designers, again including Meier, Tigerman and Venturi. Among these designs there were unmistakable references to art deco in both its cubist influenced and streamlined phases. Striking among the Alessi silver was Michael Graves' tea service which evoked art deco in an idiosyncratic and architectonic way with exaggerated shapes like those of his lounge chair.

Steuben Glass had continued to produce all along, on demand, its 1930s art deco designs by Sidney Waugh and others, but a recent design by Paul Schulze, *New York, New York*, reiterated basic art deco themes and interests. The block of solid crystal, whose corners were carved out

Above: Sharp QT-50 stereo radio cassette recorder, 1984.

Above: Stanley Tigerman, 'Sunshine' china, 1984.

in the shapes of the Woolworth, Chrysler, Empire State and World Trade Center buildings, referred not only to the popular skyscraper style of the 1920s, but also exploited the prismatic, refractive quality of crystal to achieve a cubist-like fragmentation of light and images. The use of light as an expressive design element echoed historical art deco's interest in innovative lighting effects, such as the nighttime illumination of the exterior of zigzag style skyscrapers, and in the experimentation with lighting at the world's fairs of the 1930s.

In the field of contemporary industrial design, the art deco revival also had an impact. In 1984, the Sharp corporation introduced a stereo radio cassette recorder in streamlined molded plastic, complete with encircling speed stripes. This appliance was available in white, reminiscent of 1930s Hollywood design, and in a pink and a turquoise echoing the hues of tropical deco. And the Airstream company, which had continued to produce its silvery streamlined trailers through the decades, produced in the 1980s a similarly streamlined motor home, whose aerodynamic shape paralleled both the DC-8 airplanes and streamlined locomotives of the 1930s.

Environmental designers also utilized art deco motifs for major projects. A prime example was the 1984 Los Angeles Olympics which relied primarily on already existing athletic facilities, including the classical moderne style stadium constructed for the 1932 Los Angeles Olympics. These diverse sites were unified by an inclusive graphic design program created by Sussman/Prezja & Company and the Jerde Partnership architects. With the use of brightly hued geometric shapes and patterns, and scaffolding, paper, textiles and stock industrial parts, the sports spectacular was transformed at low cost into an ephemeral art deco/constructivist fantasy.

An environmental project of a far more limited scope was painter Richard Haas' inventive recreation of a trompe-l'oeil art deco interior, executed for a New York gallery. A convincing illusionistic evocation of a luxurious 1920s zigzag style interior, the room was intended partially as a homage to the past, as well as a plea for the preservation of America's rich art deco heritage. For his illusionistic mural projects, the eclectic Haas drew on a diversity of historical styles – ranging from classicism to the work of Louis Sullivan.

Exterior designers also drew on art deco to recreate glamorous and nostalgic settings for fashionable restaurants, bars, hotels, and even buildings undergoing conversion to condominiums. This effect was often achieved by incorporating authentic historical art deco architectural elements – such as sculpture, doors, stained glass windows, etched glass, signs, and even entire rooms – which had been saved from destroyed buildings. Thus it is not surprising, for example, to find a recycled art deco Loew's Theater neon marquee as a dramatic bar centerpiece, or to see two art deco stone eagles from New York City's demolished Airlines Terminal Building flanking the main entrance of Best Product headquarters in Richmond, Virginia.

Architecture, as is customarily the case, was the most conservative of the design arts. But as the ideas of Robert Venturi gained adherents and as International Style architecture increasingly came to be seen as anti-humanistic and visually sterile, pluralism in architectural design gradually gained acceptance. The eclectic designs in which color, ornament, and historicism played an often symbolic or ironic role were grouped under the inclusive title of Postmodernism. A pioneer in the reintroduction of art deco design elements into the contemporary architectural vocabulary was Michael Graves. During the mid 1970s, Graves' previously International Style designs gave way to a more ornamented architecture which alluded to various historical styles. His 1977 private dance studio, for example, incorporated 1930s style speed stripes, but applied in an asymmetrical fashion and on a building that was not streamlined. The building also suggested other art deco elements – the use of bright colors, a simplified monumentality, and skyscraper style setbacks. Graves' fondness for art deco also extended to interior design, as seen in the skyscraper style tile pattern for the guest bath in his own residence.

By the mid 1980s, the flat topped monolithic slabs and boxes that had dominated the American skyline in the decades after World War II began to be joined by new skyscrapers and other major buildings reminiscent of the art deco era – such as the stepped KOIN Center skyscraper by the Zimmer Gunsul Frasca Partnership in Portland, Oregon, and Seattle's Bagley Wright Theatre by the NBBJ Group in a streamlined style with red speed stripes, porthole vents, and a red neon sculpture on the stepped façade. Other projects included a new Los Angeles Filmcorp Center in the form of a colossal streamlined ziggurat, and diverse Postmodern stepped skyscrapers with decorated tops and embellished bases. Thus American art deco, whose most splendid monuments were the zigzag style skyscrapers of the 1920s, had come full circle in influencing a new generation of urban skyscrapers erected over half a century later.

SELECTED BIBLIOGRAPHY

General

Bush, Donald J. *The Streamlined Decade.* New York: George Braziller, 1975.

Clark, Robert Judson, et al. *Design in America: The Cranbrook Vision 1925-1950.* New York: Harry N. Abrams, 1983.

Darling, Sharon S. *Chicago Ceramics and Glass.* Chicago: Chicago Historical Society, 1979.

Davies, Karen. *At Home in Manhattan: Modern Decorative Arts, 1925 to the Depression.* New Haven: Yale University Art Gallery, 1983.

Gebhard, David and Von Breton, Harriet. *Kem Weber: The Moderne in Southern California.* University of California-Santa Barbara, 1976.

Greif, Martin. *Depression Modern.* New York: Universe Books, 1975.

Hillier, Bevis. *The World of Art Deco.* New York: E. P. Dutton, 1971.

Kingsbury, Martha. *Art of the Thirties – The Pacific Northwest.* Seattle: University of Washington Press, 1972.

Meikle, Jeffrey L. *Twentieth Century Limited.* Philadelphia: Temple University Press, 1979.

Weiss, Peg. *The Art Deco Environment.* Syracuse: Everson Museum of Art, 1976.

Sources and Parallels

Fleischmann, Laura J. and Tepper, Marjorie. *Margaret Bourke-White: The Deco Lens.* Syracuse University: Joe and Emily Lowe Art Gallery, 1978.

Greenwood, Michael. *Art Deco Tendencies in Canadian Painting.* Toronto: Art Gallery of York University, 1977.

Rutgers University Art Gallery. *Vanguard American Sculpture, 1913-1939.* New Brunswick, N.J.: Rutgers University, 1979.

Tsujimoto, Karen. *Images of America: Precisionist Painting and Modern Photography.* Seattle: University of Washington Press, 1982.

Architecture

Balfour, Alan. *Rockefeller Center: Architecture as Theater.* New York: McGraw Hill, 1978.

Cerwinske, Laura. *Tropical Deco, The Architecture and Design of Old Miami Beach.* New York: Rizzoli, 1981.

Craig, Lois, et al. *The Federal Presence.* Cambridge: MIT Press, 1978.

Ferriss, Hugh. *The Metropolis of Tomorrow.* New York: Washburn, 1929.

Gebhard, David. *L.A. in the Thirties.* Los Angeles: Peregrine Smith, Inc., 1975.

— *The Richfield Building, 1928-1968.* New York: Atlantic Richfield Co., 1968.

— *Tulsa Art Deco.* Tulsa, Oklahoma: The Junior League of Tulsa, Inc., 1980.

Hitchcock, Henry-Russell and Seale, William. *Temples of Democracy.* New York: Harcourt Brace Jovanovich, 1976.

Jacoby, Stephen M. *Architectural Sculpture in New York City.* New York: Dover, 1975.

Jolly, Ellen Roy and Calhoun, James. *The Louisiana Capitol, Baton Rouge.* Gretna, Louisiana: Pelican Publishing Co., 1980.

Karp, Walter. *The Center: A History and Guide to Rockefeller Center.* New York: Van Nostrand Reinhold, 1983.

Krinsky, Carol Herselle. *Rockefeller Center.* New York: Oxford University Press, 1978.

Lebovich, William. *America's City Halls.* Washington, D.C.: The Preservation Press, 1984.

Robinson, Cervin and Bletter, Rosemary Haag. *Skyscraper Style: Art Deco New York.* New York: Oxford University Press, 1975.

Robinson, Karalyn, et al. *Portfolio: Art Deco Historic District, Miami Beach.* Miami Beach: Bucolo Preservation Press, 1979.

Short, Charles Wilkins. *Public Works Administration Public Buildings, 1933-1939.* Washington: U.S. Government Printing Office, 1939.

Stone, Susannah. *The Oakland Paramount.* Berkeley, California: Lancaster Miller, 1982.

University of Cincinnati. *Art Deco and the Cincinnati Union Terminal*, 1973.

Varian, Elayne H. *American Art Deco Architecture.* New York: Finch College Museum of Art, 1975.

Whiffen, Marcus and Breeze, Carla. *Pueblo Deco: The Art Deco Architecture of the Southwest.* Albuquerque: University of New Mexico Press, 1984.

Furniture and Interior Design

Darling, Sharon S. *Chicago Furniture.* Chicago Historical Society in association with W. W. Norton, New York, 1984.

Emery, Marc. *Furniture by Architects.* New York: Harry N. Abrams, 1983.

Frankl, Paul. *Form and Re-form.* New York: Harper, 1930.

— *Machine-Made Leisure.* New York: Harper, 1932.

— *New Dimensions.* New York: Payson and Clarke, 1928.

Hanks, David A. *The Decorative Designs of Frank Lloyd Wright.* New York: E. P. Dutton, 1979.

— *Innovative Furniture in America From 1800 to the Present.* New York: Horizon Press, 1981.

Illustration and Graphic Art

Bader, Barbara. *American Picture Books from Noah's Ark to the Beast Within.* New York: Macmillan, 1976.

Johnson, Fridolf and Gorton, John F. H. *The Illustrations of Rockwell Kent.* New York: Dover, 1976.

Shire, Sanford. *Nelle.* New York: Rizzoli, 1981.

Vassos, John. *Contempo, Phobia and Other Graphic Interpretations.* New York: Dover, 1976.

Ceramics, Glass, Metalware, Plastics

Clark, Garth. *A Century of Ceramics in the United States, 1878-1978.* New York: E. P. Dutton, 1979.

Dinoto, Andrea. *Art Plastic: Designed for Living.* New York: Abbeville, 1984.

Florence, Gene. *The Collectors Encyclopedia of Depression Glass.* Paducah, Kentucky: Collector Books, 1979.

Henzke, Lucile. *American Art Pottery.* New York: Thomas Nelson, 1970.

Katz, Sylvia. *Plastics: Common Objects, Classic Designs.* New York: Harry N. Abrams, 1984.

Klamkin, Marian. *The Collectors Guide to Depression Glass.* New York: Hawthorne Books, 1973.

Postle, Kathleen R. *The Chronicle of Overbeck Pottery.* Indianapolis: Indiana Historical Society, 1978.

Washington State University. *Noritake Art Deco Porcelains: Collection of Howard Kottler.* Pullman: Washington State University, 1982.

Industrial Design

Cheney, Sheldon and Martha. *Art and the Machine.* New York: McGraw-Hill, 1936.

Dreyfuss, Henry. *Designing for People.* Reprint. New York: Viking Press, 1974 [1955].

Geddes, Norman Bel. *Horizons.* Reprint. New York: Dover, 1977 [1932].

— *Magic Motorways.* New York: Random House, 1940.

Hennessey, William J. *Russel Wright: American Designer.* Cambridge: MIT Press, 1983.

Pulos, Arthur J. *American Design Ethic.* Cambridge: MIT Press, 1983.

Teague, Walter Dorwin. *Design This Day.* New York: Harcourt, Brace, 1940.

New Deal Art Programs

Berman, Greta. *The Lost Years: Painting in New York City Under the Works Progress Administration Federal Art Project.* New York: Garland, 1979.

McKinzie, Richard D. *The New Deal for Artists*. Princeton University Press, 1973.

Marling, Karal Ann. *Wall-to-Wall America*. Minneapolis: University of Minnesota Press, 1982.

O'Connor, Francis V. (ed.). *Art for the Millions*. Greenwich, Ct.: New York Graphic Society, 1973.

— *The New Deal Projects: An Anthology of Memoirs*. Washington, D.C.: Smithsonian Institution, 1972.

Park, Marlene and Markowitz, Gerald E. *New Deal for Art*. Hamilton, N.Y.: Gallery Association of New York State, 1977.

Expositions

Applebaum, Stanley. *The New York World's Fair 1939/1940*. New York: Dover, 1977.

Corn, Joseph J. and Horrigan, Brian. *Yesterday's Tomorrows: Past Visions of the American Future*. New York: Summit Books, 1984.

Harrison, Helen A. *Dawn of a New Day, The New York World's Fair, 1939/40*. New York: The Queens Museum and New York University Press, 1980.

ACKNOWLEDGMENTS

Academy of Motion Picture Arts and Sciences 40
Collection, Albany Institute of History and Art 91
Arizona Biltmore Hotel 6, 56 top, 57 top
Arkitektura 76 top right, 78 both, 185 all
The Arrow Co 90
Art Gallery of Ontario, Toronto 94
Art Institute of Chicago, Collection AIC Federal Art Project 42 right; Gift of the Antiquarian Society through Mrs Philip K Wrigley Fund 70; Gifts of Fred A Goldberg and Harvey A Goldberg 84 top two; Gift of Mr and Mrs Hugh J Smith Jr 127 top
Association of American Railroads 142, 169 bottom
Auburn Cord Deusenberg Museum 139 bottom
B & O Railroad Museum 64 top
Don Beatty 146, 150-51, 151
Angela Bertinetti 67 top
Marcello Bertinetti 11, 34 bottom, 159 top
Jeff Bleckman 2, 23, 50, 53 top, 131 both, 134 both
Bruce Boehner 10, 14-15 both, 18, 55 both, 56 bottom, 57 bottom, 58, 62, 62-63
Ron Boff 99
Steven Brooke 22-23, 67 bottom, 139 top
John Calabrese 34 top left, 51 both, 54 left, 66
California College of Arts and Crafts, Oakland/Sinel Papers 133
Chicago Historical Society 75 top right and bottom left
Christies, NYC 16 top left, 72 bottom, 73 right, 75 top left, 76 top left, 77 top left, 79 all 3, 83 top, 86, 128 top
The Chronicle of the Overbeck Pottery, Kathleen Postle 108 bottom
The Chrysler Museum, Norfolk, VA 86 bottom
The Coca Cola Bottling Co 65
Collector Books, KY 125, 126 both, 127 bottom
Cooper-Hewitt Museum, The Smithsonian Institution's National Museum of Design 95 both
Cowan Pottery Museum, Ohio/Larry L Peltz 110,

111 bottom right
Cranbrook Academy of Art/Museum 74, 87, 112 right
A Richard DeNatale 130 left and below right
Eastman Kodak Co 143 bottom
Elements Gallery, NYC 183 both, 184
Everson Museum of Art, Syracuse NY 53 bottom; Gift of International Business Machines Corp 109 right; Gift of an Anonymous Friend of the Artist 114
Fifty-50 Gallery, NYC 98, 130 top right
FPG/E Powell 159 bottom
Gallery Association of NY 148 top, 149, 156
Garth Clark Gallery, LA/NY 109 left, 116
General Electric Co 145 top, 164, 165 bottom, 166, 169 top
General Motors 167, 177
Collection of George Mason University, Fairfax, VA 102 both
The George Walter Vincent Smith Art Museum, Gift of Irma Kirkham 176 bottom
Gorham-Textron 128 bottom
Greater Baton Rouge Chamber of Commerce 61 both
Hirshhorn Museum and Sculpture Garden, Smithsonian Institution 13
Hopkins Studio, Tulsa, OK 49 bottom, 54 right
Howard University, Moorland-Spingard Research Center, Collection of Mary O'H Williamson 97
International Contract Furnishings Inc 82 top left
International Museum of Photography at George Eastman House, Rochester, NY 44
Johnson Wax 68 top, 83 bottom
Jordan Volpe Gallery, NYC 71
Wade H Knight Photogrphy, Texas 108 top
Howard Kottler 106, 115 both, 118
Schecter Lee/ESTO 111 top two, bottom left, 119 all, 135 top two

Leo Castelli Gallery (Eric Pollitzer) 180
John Margolies/ESTO 19, 138, 143 top, 160
The Metropolitan Museum of Art 72 top, 80, 81 both, 162; Gift of Juliette B Castle and Mrs Paul Dahlstrom 16 top right; Gift of Charles Bregler 41; Gift of Paul Outerbridge 43; Emil Blasberg Memorial Fund 77 below; Edward C Moore Jr, gifts 112 left, 124; Gift of Mrs Hunt Slater 117; The Chase Foundation Inc and Edgar Kaufman gifts 129
Minnesota Historical Society 17 top
Montclair Art Museum, NJ 29
The Museum of Modern Art, NY, Walter J Reinemann Fund 37 bottom; Gift of Joseph Binder 103 top left; Gift of the Office for Emergency Management 104; Gift of Lester Beall 105
The Museum of Modern Art/Film Stills Archive 4-5, 16 bottom, 17 bottom, 20, 21, 89 top
National Film Archive/Stills Library, London 100-01
National Gallery of Art 26
National Museum of American Art, Smithsonian Institution, Gift of the Estate of Paul Manship 33
National Park Service 39 below
National Trust for Historic Preservation 12, 89 bottom
New York Central System 49 top
New York Public Library Picture Collection 165 top, 167 bottom, 168, 170-71, 172 top, 173 both, 174, 175, 176 top
New York Public Library at Lincoln Center, Billy Rose Theater Collection 103 top right
The Newark Museum 28, 36 both
Francis V O'Connor 157
Oregon Dept of Transportation 161
Emmy Lou Packard 152-53

INDEX

MAR '87

DATE DUE

OCT 25 '88			
NOV 22 '88			
NOV 0 3 2008			
SEP 2 1 2013			
Dec 1, 2013